SHIVBA

The childhood of Maharaja Shivaji

Vikrant Shivaji Shinde

Sivitra Publications

ISBN: 978-93-6039-877-4

For Rivansh & Avnir

CONTENTS

ACKNOWLEDGMENTS

There could not be a bigger and higher force than the mighty Sahyadri which has motivated me to write this book. For the one like me who has grown up in Sahyadri region, listening to the legends of the brave warriors and anecdotes surrounding Shivba is very common. This book would not have been possible without the historians like Ninad Bedekar, for his speeches and books, Pandurang Balkawade, for his research and speeches, Jadunath Sarkar, through his book *'Shivaji and his times'*, Babasaheb Purandare, who dedicated his life for it and others who have told history like never before. The guiding light of invaluable work of *Shri Shiv Bharat* composed by Kavindra Parmanand Newaskar under the command of Chhatrapati Shivaji Maharaj himself, still serves as the most reliable source of history. Bharat Itihas Sanshodhak Mandal as an institute stands at the epicenter as a great source of historical research. I extend my heartfelt thanks to the precious contributions of various *Bakhars,* relentless efforts of *Shiv Shahirs*, and such other unknown torch-bearers of Maratha history whom we do not know of.

I. INTRODUCTION

The greatest-ever warrior to take birth in the Indian subcontinent was Chhatrapati Shivaji Maharaj. Shivaji is the name of this warrior king and in India, the one who was a great king in older times, was called a Maharaj. That's how the name came into being. 'Chhatrapati' is a Sanskrit language work which is a combination of *Chhatra* (shelter or umbrella) and *pati* (master/ruler). He was phenomenal in his skills in warfare, administration, and diplomacy. But he was a humble, religious and extremely moral human being.

There have thousands of kings and hundreds of emperors, then the question lies that why Shivba is so highly regarded by people especially in India and in many parts of the world. It is good and reasonable to carry out this inspection and question as to whether he was really great or are people driven by just their sentiments about him. It is not very difficult to find this answer. The historical evidences dating back at least three hundred and forty-four years from his death, show that there lived a man of valour and integrity of such epic proportions that there was none other who replaced him from that epitome.

Shivba's life journey was challenging in all respects, be it personal or political but the way he surmounted all his difficulties has deeply motivated generations to follow his footsteps. We may not do complete justice to trail his path, but the least we can do is take one step in the direction shown by him that will lead us towards justice, equality and morality as a being. He taught us how to achieve independence, how to keep it and how not to lose the independence to any external force. Independence has a subjective meaning which kept on changing over the years but the essence of it would always remain the same. Today we may not be so worried about the Independence of our country as much as we would be about our safety, self-sufficiency and self-reliance. That is the subjective shift of meaning of values in the context of what is to be learned from Shivba.

Shivba is, no doubt, highly revered among the masses but he is open to assessment and evaluation for his values with an equitable application of logic and reasoning. Some ancient texts have described him to be an incarnation of Lord Vishnu as he possessed all the features of a saviour as an avatar, a chance of possibility validated by occurrence of near-divine events surrounding his life. Whether he was an avatar or he wasn't, it makes no difference, as far as we see the moral of his story.

Several universities around the world teach about his warfare, certain naval establishments hail him for his naval accomplishments. He is considered the 'Father of Indian Navy' for bringing in the navy warfare and rebuilding it from scratch. His administration skills have found global admirers and his robust and transparent justice system has no parallel.

Ho Chi Minh served as Vietnamese President for more than two decades and served as nationalist movement leader for three decades. He led the war against United States for nearly twenty years and inflicted huge losses to the powerful enemy with guerrilla tactics. Ho Chi Minh had claimed to be personally inspired by Shivba's guerrilla warfare which Vietnamese had studied for their conflict with United States. Shivba has been consistently recognized on international arena as the people learned about him and were fascinated by his brilliant statesmanship.

There is a lot of literature, paintings, powada or ballads, stories, motion pictures on the rise and rise of

Shivba. He was a brave warrior, obedient son, ideal husband, great friend but above all a person who is admired by people after three hundred and forty-four years, a generation far off from the one he belonged to.

This story starts much earlier to the birth of Shivba, depicting the situation hundreds of years before him and pauses, although not conclude, at his oath of establishing a just and rightful kingdom for his subjects, Swarajya. It does not intend to overlook his humility with poor and the loving side of his personality. Shivba's brilliance and his art of fortification are evident from the historical records and forts that speak for themselves. Although here the focus is on his childhood and how he grew up, the narrative of his respect for women, a chapter very relevant in today's circumstances, is imperative as well as timeless.

The deities are worshipped in Hinduism who incarnated on earth and established the rule of Sanatan Dharma. But Dharma has to be protected by the unflinching hands of strong-willed men and women. It would not be an overstatement to say that there would not have been Hinduism, as it has been, if Shivba had not been born. At the times of forceful conversions and religious fanatic persecutions of Hindus at the hands of Islamic invaders, Shivba stood as immovable rock in the way of evil and restored Dharma on this land.

Mahakavi (great poet) Bhushan composed a poem which has a Quatrain saying:

पीरा पयगम्बरा दिगम्बरा दिखाई देत,
सिद्ध की सिधाई गई, रही बात रब की।
कासी हूँ की कला गई मथुरा मसीत भई
शिवाजी न होतो तो सुनति होती सबकी।

(Islamic prophet started seeming holy,
Enlightened are appearing to be frail,
Kashi's culture would vanish;
Mathura would turn into Mosque,
If Shivaji wouldn't exist, we shall have converted)

1. BHARATVARSH

ततश्च भारतं वर्षमेतल्लोकेषुगीयते।
भरताय यत: पित्रा दत्तं प्रतिष्ठिता वनम्॥
(विष्णु पुराण, २,१,३२)

This country is known as Bhāratavarṣa since the times the father entrusted the kingdom to the son Bharata and he himself went to the forest for ascetic practices.
–Vishnu Purana (2, 1, 32)

Bharatvarsha or Bhārata is the name of India and other regions which were around India although the entire Earth is called Bharatvarsha in the Brahmand's scriptural descriptions. The entire nation was given the name Bharatvarsha after the ancient Bharata tribe. Bharatvarsha means land of the Bharata who was the ancestor of *Pandavas* and *Kauravas*. The other texts refer to the region south of the Himalayas as Bharatvarsha. Another name for Bharat is *Aryavarta* and according to the Rig Veda, the people who live in Aryavarta are called Aryans. The Sindhu River was referred to as Hindu by the Persians, and as a result, Hindustan was created. Due to the English naming of the Sindhu River as the Indus, Hindustan became known as India. Jambudvīpa ('Berry Island') was used in ancient scriptures as a name of India before the term Bhārata became widespread.

India (or Bharat as it is) was once known as a 'Golden Bird'. It was because of the prosperity and wealth it had. It was the center of trade and commerce. India has the mighty Himalayas in the north and it is bordered by sea on the south. The presence of sea has greatly helped in the spreading of business across the world.

The people in India worship the nature. They even have their holy places close to nature, such as Kailash Mansarovar, Badrinath, Kedarnath, Gangotri, Yamnotri. Amarnath is situated in the icy cave of Kashmir. The temple of Goddess in Kanyakumari is located at the tip, at land's-end in the south of India. Hardwar, which means 'Gateway to Lord Vishnu', is nestled at Himalayan foothills, where Ganga flows out into the plains. The Ganga meets Yamuna and Sarasvati at Triveni Sangam at Prayaga or Prayagraj.

The places of Mathura and Vrindaban where Krishna lived and we hear about his lovely stories. Bodh Gaya located in Magadha (now known as Bihar) where the Buddha attained enlightenment under the sacred fig tree. The holy place of Panchavati (means 'Garden of Five Banyan Trees') at Nashik in ancient Dandakaranya Forest on the banks of River Godavari, which Lord Rama and Sita made their home during their fourteen-years exile. There are many such places in Maharashtra, Kerala and Tamil Nadu.

The holy Varanasi (also once known as Benaras or Kashi) is one of the oldest continuously inhabited cities in the world. Mark Twain, the famous writer said:

"Benares is older than history, older than tradition, older even than legend, and looks twice as old as all of them put together."

India was majorly the centers of knowledge and wisdom. The oldest University in the world Takshshila University and later Nalanda University the second oldest University were in India where the students came from Korea, Japan, China, Tibet, Indonesia, Persia, Turkey and many other countries. The Scholars from all over the world came to India to learn and thrive. There was only one place where they knew the wisdom existed and that was India. Students, merchants, traders, travellers, sages, explorers, everyone wanted to come to India for its prosperity and glory, to enrich themselves with wisdom and wealth. There were other education centers like Vikramshila University, Vallabhi University, Jagaddala University, Nagarjuna Vidyapeeth and Kanthaloor University, among other few.

The American historian and philosopher Will Durant, who co-wrote a series of books with his wife Ariel Durant named 'Story of Civilization' which took them forty years to write, has recognized the contribution of India to the western civilization:

> *"India was the motherland of our race, and Sanskrit the mother of Europe's languages: she was the mother of our philosophy; mother, through the Arabs, of much of our mathematics; mother, through the Buddha, of the ideals embodied in Christianity; mother, through the village community, of self-government and democracy. Mother India is in many ways the mother of us all."*

Mark Twain, the famous writer, famously said:

> *"India is the cradle of the human race, the birthplace of human speech, the mother of history, the grandmother of legend and the great-grand mother of tradition."*

Albert Einstein said in acknowledging contribution of India to world civilization:

"We owe a lot to the Indians, who taught us how to count, without which no worthwhile scientific discovery could have been made."

India is the mother of all civilizations and that is because all other civilizations have arisen from India. India had an advanced civilization right when other countries were still primitive. The Indus Valley Civilization (also known as the Indus Civilization), was a Bronze Age civilization in India, lasting from 3300 BCE to 1300 BCE, with most famous sites of Mohenjo-Daro and Harappa. India is a treasure of the world where one can find the traditional, cultural and ancient scientific values.

During the ancient times, India was not only the leading exporter of silk, sugar, cotton, precious stones but also the major exporter of spices to the west and this was carried through the Spice Route. The trade routes connecting the East and the West were known as the Silk Route (land route) and the Spice route (sea route). The Silk and Spice routes passed through different trade centers. The Silk Route was a historic trade route stretched from Asia to the Mediterranean, crossing China, India, Persia, Arabia, Greece, and Italy. Spice Route was the network of sea routes from which the Spices, generally very expensive, were taken from the East to the West by traders and merchants, to be sold at insanely high prices in European markets. The Spice Route (also known as Maritime Silk Roads) stretches from the west coast of Japan, through the islands of Indonesia, around India to the lands of the Middle East, and from there, across the Mediterranean to Europe. It is a distance of over fifteen thousand kilometers which the Spice and other exports covered to reach their destinations. All these items were exported in exchange for gold and silver from traders and merchants of other countries.

India was the leading business centre of the world and commercial towns like Harappa and Mohenjo-Daro were established. In ancient times, India had built strong business relations with other countries like Mesopotamia and trade took place between the two nations involving gold, silver, terracotta pots, precious stones, and pearls. Trade and commerce played a significant role in the economic strength and thus the political powers in India. It was evident from the archaeological evidence that trade and commerce through land and sea played a very important role in the prosperity and growth of India.

India had become a melting pot of cultures as many European, Dutch, French, Arabian and other travellers frequented India. The Hindu mercantile community was popular for their entrepreneurship, nature of enterprising, resilience and for being trustworthy. Goods manufactured in India were excellent and unique and could not be found in any other part of the world. The Hindus were very skilled at the art of building ships as they had superior knowledge of the sea routes, winds and other aspects of navigation. These were a key to enabling themselves to travel distant lands to conduct trade.

India is not just another country that exists in this world. It is a mother of civilization and has a huge history owing to its existence for thousands of years or in short till when it could be traced back. The richness of its historic value is beyond any measure. The traces of its vast history can be seen in its two epics, Ramayana and Mahabharata.

Ramayana: The First Epic

Ramayana is a historical account of the seventh incarnation of Lord Vishnu as '*Ram*' put into words by *Sage Valmiki* around seven thousand years ago. The Ramayana is a revered Hindu scripture that tells the story of Lord Rama, his wife *Sita*, his brother *Lakshmana* and his loyal devotee *Hanuman*. The epic is divided into seven Kandas (books) and explores themes of duty, righteousness, devotion, and the triumph of good over evil.

There is an interesting background why Valmiki wrote Ramayana. Ratnakar, as he was originally named, took birth in a noble Brahmin family. He fell in to bad company and chose evil ways which turned him into a robber. Once a sage passed by him who advised him to turn good. The sage said that the sins he amassed through such a low life had to be corrected somehow

Ratnakar went home and told his wife and children that he was involved in the robbery only for their sake. So, they share all his earnings, will they also share the sins he amassed through this evil deeds. They all instantly denied sharing the sins and said it was up to him how he earned and that they will never be able to account for the sins done by him.

This incident turned Valmiki a noble man. He resorted to self-purification and went into a deep meditation for years. A huge anthill covered him in course of time giving him the name Valmiki ('Val-Miki', Ant-Hill). Valmiki chanted the name of Sri Rama which transformed him into a noble soul. His austere life and devotion made him a great scholar and a singer.

Once when he was strolling in the quiet forest enjoying nature, he heard a couple of birds happily singing. Suddenly, a hunter emerged and shot at the female bird which fell down dead causing agony to the other bird. Valmiki was moved by this pitiable sight and cursed the hunter for causing the grief. The curse took a form of a first Sanskrit verse of Ramayana. Valmiki later repented for cursing him. Meanwhile, Lord Brahma appeared in front of him and said he need not worry due to his act since it was divinely inspired by him. It was destined that Valmiki should compose the great epic of Ramayana, the story of Sri Rama's noble life and accomplishments on this earth. In fact, the curse from his lips became the first verse of the epic and made him the first poet or Adi Kavi, and Ramayana became the first poem or Kaavya.

The story begins with the birth of Rama, the seventh avatar of Lord Vishnu, and his childhood adventures. Rama is married to Sita, who is an incarnation of the goddess Lakshmi. Their happiness, however, is short-lived when Rama is unjustly banished for fourteen years from the kingdom of Ayodhya accompanied by his devoted wife Sita and loyal brother Lakshmana. Kaikeyi's son Bharata swore never to ascend the throne as it was his older brother's birthright and he remained as a regent till Rama returned from his exile.

In the garden of Panchavati, Sita is abducted by the demon king Ravana. Rama and Lakshmana embark on a perilous journey to Lanka, the kingdom of Ravana, to rescue Sita. Rama and Lakshmana receive help from various allies, including the monkey-god Hanuman and an army of monkeys led by Sugriva and Angada. A big war ensues between Rama's army of vanaras (monkeys) and Ravana's demon forces in Lanka. Hanuman and his allies help Rama defeat Ravana and rescue Sita.

Ramayana is not just a tale of heroism and adventure but it serves as a moral and philosophical guide, teaching the importance of Dharma (righteousness) and the Karma (the good or bad effect of doing something). The epic continues to inspire generations for thousands of years, shaping cultural and moral values in Hinduism and other traditions.

Mahabharata: The Second Epic

The epic of Mahabharata is an extraordinary one. Krishna, the eighth incarnation of Lord Vishnu, lived at the time of Mahabharat. In the ancient India five thousand years ago, there existed a grand kingdom named Hastinapura, ruled by King Dhritarashtra. The kin of King Dhritarashtra and his brother Pandu lead into two sets of cousins; the virtuous Pandavas, and the cunning Kauravas. Pandavas were five brothers who had Draupadi as a wife and Kauravas, were hundred brothers and one sister, Dussala, born to King Dhritarashtra and Gandhari.

The eldest of Kauravas, Duryodhana, was envious of the Pandavas' popularity, especially their brave and skillful leader, Yudhishthira since their childhood. Duryodhana's jealousy grew as they grew older, leading to an ill-fated wicked game of dice, where he deceitfully snatched the Pandavas' kingdom and banished them to exile for thirteen years.

After their exile, the Pandavas returned and claimed their rightful kingdom. Lord Krishna, who was a divine guide to Pandavas, tried to bring peace between the Pandavas and Kauravas. Pandavas wanted only five villages, namely, *Panipat, Sonipat, Baghpat, Indraprastha, and Tilpat* but Duryodhana, blinded by his ego and greed, refused to give away as much land as was covered by the point of a needle, let alone the five villages proposed by Krishna. Peace efforts failed, and war became inevitable. The stage was set for the great Kurukshetra war, a battle that would determine the fate of the historical events that followed.

The Pandavas were noble and just, but the Kauravas were arrogant, jealous and power-hungry. The two sides gathered their allies and prepared for the epic battle. Krishna gave a choice to Arjuna and Duryodhana, between Krishna himself, unarmed and would not pick up any weapon, and his army called Narayani Sena, to be on their side in the battle. Arjuna, who got the first turn, chose Krishna. Duryodhana was happy and thought Arjuna to be a fool for not choosing his Narayani Sena. The Pandavas army, led by Yudhishthira, Bhima, Arjuna, Nakula, and Sahadeva, faced Duryodhana and his brothers leading the Kauravas army. The battlefield of Kurukshetra was immense and severe, filled with brave warriors, powerful elephants, and chariots and led to a massive slaughter.

Lord Krishna, amidst the colossal chaos, the divine incarnation, served as Arjuna's charioteer and guide. Pandavas prince Arjuna, the great archer was torn by doubt and moral dilemma on the eve of battle looking at his own people as enemies. He was hesitant to fight against his own blood, friends and Guru (teacher) on the other side. In his moment of dilemmatic crisis, Arjuna sought Krishna's divine guidance. Krishna, with infinite wisdom, imparted the teachings of duty and righteousness, known as the Bhagavad Gita, to Arjuna. Krishna told Arjuna about dharma (righteousness) and karma (action) and encouraged Arjuna to fulfill his duty without attachment to the outcome. Krishna's words inspired and strengthened Arjuna who resolved to fight for justice and righteousness.

The battle of Kurukshetra ensued, and the war raged on for eighteen days while the battlefield echoed with the clash of warriors and their powerful weapons. The trumpeting of elephants and the deafening war cries inspired the warriors to fight till their end.

Warriors from both the sides fought valiantly, displaying extraordinary valour and will. The Pandavas and their army, guided by Krishna's wisdom, fought with fortitude and righteousness.

Krishna, the Lord himself, advised and supported the Pandavas by helping them in the strategic decisions, ensuring that justice reigned. The battle was fierce and brutal; leading to huge loss of life and destruction but the hardships could not stop the Pandavas who remained unfaltering for the sake of their righteousness.

The Pandavas, at the end, became victorious, but the victory came at a great price of devastation. The historical account of Mahabharata serves as a timeless lesson, teaching the importance of righteousness, moral values, and the consequences of ill will, greed and arrogance. Lord Krishna's teachings in Bhagavad Gita show the significance of duty, devotion, and selfless action when there is an adversity. The epic of Mahabharata stands as a symbol of wisdom and virtue, teaching generations the eternal truths of life, for thousands of years.

2. BIRTH OF A HERO

The birth of our Hero, Shivba, cannot be understood unless we know what ensued for centuries before his birth. It is only then we can understand why his birth and life was so significantly impactful for the entire sub-continent. India or Bharat is a sub-continent of rich heritage, vast history and unbelievable geology which is unparalleled in the whole world. India has spectacular features that catalyzed the process of evolution of humans which later shaped into prominent civilizations. This led to the fact that India assumed the motherhood of civilizations which exists even today.

The historians have classified various time periods of time or epochs, Stone Age, Copper Age, Bronze Age and Iron Age. The characteristic of an Iron Age culture is the mass production of tools and weapons made not just of found iron, but from steel alloys as well. Some really major and prominent empires existed in India before and during Iron Age. We will consider the empires in Iron Age which had lasting impact on the Indian sub-continent and subsequently on the geopolitics of the sub-continent.

Maurya Empire (322 BCE - 185 BCE)

Mauryan Empire was founded by Chandragupta Maurya; this was one of the largest and most powerful empires in ancient in Magadha, India. Chandragupta Maurya defeated Dhana Nanda, the last ruler of Nanda Empire and established the Maurya Empire that lasted for one hundred and thirty-six years. The rise of Mauryan Empire is hugely credited to the chief royal advisor Chanakya or Kautilya, who was a teacher, author, strategist, philosopher, economist and jurist. He authored *Arthashastra*, a treatise or formal book statecraft, political science, economic policy, military strategy and Hindu philosophy which is regarded as relevant even today. Chanakya was a scholar at Takshashila University along with and Chandragupta Maurya with the students like Panini, Sanskrit grammarian, Charaka, the ancient physician.

Chandragupta's son Bindusara reigned for twenty-five years and consolidated the empire built by his father. Bindusara's elder and favourite son *Susima* was a rightful heir to his throne but when Bindusara died, Ashoka ascended to the throne by killing Susima and his other several brothers.

Under the rule of Ashoka, the Maurya Empire expanded significantly and played a crucial role in spreading Buddhism across India and beyond. Ashoka was a cruel king who killed hundreds of people just out of his rage. He had built a torture chamber disguised as a beautiful palace with exclusive baths, decorated with flowers, where he tortured people till their miserable death. Ashoka later converted to Buddhism and renounced violence. *Ashokavadana*, A Sanskrit text written by Buddhist monks from Mathura region called Ashoka as '*Chandashoka*' ('Ashoka the fierce'), and gave a detailed account of his cruel acts.

Gupta Empire (c. 240 CE - 550 CE)

The Gupta Empire is called as Golden Age of India, known for flourishing arts, science, and culture. The Gupta rulers were patrons of literature, art, and learning, who made advancements in mathematics, astronomy, and medicine.

Gupta Empire was founded by an earliest known ruler called Gupta. Gupta was succeeded by his son, Ghatotkacha, followed by Ghatotkacha's son, Chandragupta I. Chandragupta I expanded the Gupta empire who can be majorly attributed to his marriage to the Licchavi princess Kumaradevi who helped him extend his political power. Their son Samudragupta further expanded the Gupta empire and remained undefeated during his entire reign and is considered one of the greatest emperors of India in those times.

Samudragupta's son Chandragupta II, also known by his title Vikramaditya, as well as Chandragupta Vikramaditya, was the third ruler of the Gupta Empire in India, and was strongest emperor in the Gupta Empire. Vikramaditya continued the expansionist policy of his father Samudragupta, mainly through military conquests and captured the region from the Indus River in the west to the Bengal region in the east, and from the Himalayan foothills in the north to the Narmada River in the south. The Gupta Empire reached its pinnacle during the rule of Vikramaditya. The Chinese pilgrim Faxian, who visited India during his reign, suggests that he ruled over a peaceful and prosperous kingdom. The noted Sanskrit poet Kalidasa, revered for his great work in poetry and playwright primarily based on Hindu Puranas and philosophy, was his court poet.

Chola Empire (c. 300 BCE - 1279 CE)

Chola Empire is the most significant empire of the Ancient South India. They ruled for nearly fifteen hundred years and asserted their power which influenced religion, culture, and architecture. They built a sophisticated maritime trade system that extended from India throughout Southeast Asia and even to China in those times. Chola kings invested in art, literature, education, and architecture and built massive stone temples which served as cultural and social hubs. The architectures were adorned with magnificent sculptures and beautiful paintings. They were probably the first to design man-made lakes to alleviate droughts and provide a supply of safe drinking water. The Cholas were influential in South and Southeast Asia due to maritime prowess, trade, and naval achievements which helped them leave a lasting impact on the cultural and political landscape of the region.

Chola Empire was founded by Ilamchetchenni, an early Tamil king of the Chola dynasty but later it was revived by Vijayalaya Chola. Chola Empire under Rajaraja Chola I and his successors; Rajendra Chola I, Rajadhiraja Chola, Virarajendra Chola and Kulothunga Chola I, became a military and economic power in South Asia and South-East Asia. Rajendra Chola I built a new capital called Gangaikonda Cholapuram from where Cholas ruled their empire.

The year 1279 CE marked the end of the Chola Dynasty. The last Chola king, Rajendra Chola III, was defeated by Pandya king Maravarman Kulasekara

Pandyan I. The Pandyas established their rule in present day Tamil Nadu and Pandya Empire emerged which later were weakened by infighting and Islamic Invaders which ended the Pandya Empire in sixteenth Century.

Vijayanagara Empire (1336 CE - 1646 CE)

Situated in the Deccan Plateau, the Vijayanagara Empire was a major power in South India. It was known for its architectural marvels, with elaborate temples and intricate carvings. The empire played a significant role in preserving and promoting Hindu culture and traditions.

The Vijayanagara Empire was established in 1336 by Harihara I and his brother Bukka Raya I of Sangama Dynasty. The empire emerged due to culmination of attempts by the South Indian powers to fend off Islamic invasions by the end of the thirteenth century. It lasted until 1646, although its power declined after a major military defeat in 1565 in the Battle of Talikota by the combined armies of the Deccan sultanates. The Deccan sultanates were five late-medieval Indian kingdoms on the Deccan Plateau that were ruled by Muslim dynasties, namely, Ahmednagar, Berar, Bidar, Bijapur, and Golconda. The Vijaynagar empire was named after its capital city of Vijayanagara, at present day Hampi, in Karnataka, India.

The empire reached its zenith during the rule of the popular king, Krishna Deva Raya, when Vijayanagara armies were persistently undefeated. He was the third emperor of the Tuluva dynasty, and is considered to be one of the greatest rulers in South India. He ruled the largest empire in India after the fall of the Islamic Delhi Sultanate. Krishna Deva Raya defeated Bahamani Sultans, Gajapatis of Odisha and Portuguese maritime power which was rising then. Krishna Deva Raya later established friendly relations with the Portuguese in Goa in 1510 and obtained guns and Arabian horses from the Portuguese merchants. He also used Portuguese expertise to improve the water supply to the Vijayanagara capital, Hampi.

Portuguese were one of the emerging powers in the sea as were British, Dutch and French. They wanted to establish trade routes with India so they could make fortunes doing trades in huge Indian markets and selling spices, silk, jewels and other valuable goods in Europe where it had great demand. There was one such explorer called Vasco da Gama who had sailed for India in the late fifteenth century.

Vasco da Gama, the miserable explorer

Vasco da Gama, Portuguese explorer who set out in the search of India, started his exploration from

Lisbon, Portugal in 1497. Vasco da Gama's expedition was to find a direct sea route to India, which would help Portugal to bypass the heavily taxed land routes controlled by Arab and Venetian merchants. Vasco da Gama followed the sea route which was already found by earlier explorers which was through the coast of Africa. Europeans, by then were most primitive when it came to sailing and Vasco's journey for over three months sailing more than ten thousand kilometers of open-ocean was by far the longest journey out of sight of land made by any European.

King Manuel of Portugal assigned a distinctly expendable crew of convicts and criminals to go with Vasco da Gama as the chances of this voyage succeeding were rather slim. All the European explorers had not advanced beyond the southern tip of Africa, called Cape of Good Hope before so it was rather not very believable that this crew would make it to the most sought after, India. Some of Europe's claimed 'discoveries' in navigation were in fact appropriations of a well-established existing trade system in the Indian Ocean. Europeans portrayed that Indians knew only coastal navigation but they are not aware that deep-sea shipping had existed in India around two thousand years ago when Indian ships used to sail to islands such as the Andamans, Lakshadweep and Maldives. Even Kautilya who lived from 350-275 BCE describes the times that are good and bad for seafaring. Vasco da Gama was foolishly attributed by some to have discovered already thriving India, although he was only the first to discover a sea route from Portugal to India, among the fellow Europeans.

Once Vasco da Gama went around Cape of Good Hope, he reached Mozambique posing as a Muslim as he thought that local population would be hostile to a Christian. He met the Sultan of Mozambique but all he had were paltry trade goods as gifts. The population became suspicious and drove them out of Mozambique. Vasco da Gama departed the harbour, but fired the cannons in the city in feat of retaliation. There are historical accounts which say that Vasco da Gama even resorted to piracy that is, attacking ships for stealing near Mombasa where he looted Arab merchant ships that were generally unarmed. Vasco travelled a long way from Portugal and after a few halts had reached Mombasa, a coastal city in Kenya. Soon he attracted hostility with the local people and had to leave Mombasa.

Vasco da Gama further went to Malindi, Kenya on the Indian Ocean coast. There he met a Gujarati merchant cum navigation pilot, Kanji Malam who was a trader of cotton and indigo from Kutch. Kanji Malam made regular voyages to the African coast to barter his goods for gold and ivory. Kanji agreed to help Vasco da Gama as he lacked knowledge of celestial navigation and he could not navigate the Indian Ocean. Vasco needed an Indian pilot to guide him across the sea from

Malindi in Africa, to Calicut in India.

Vasco da Gama, was glorified by European historians as being one of the greatest explorers, was surprised to see that Kanji's ships were three times bigger than his own. Kanji's ships escorted the Vasco's ships across the Indian Ocean towards Kappadu, near Calicut (Kozhikode). Kanji steered Vasco da Gama across the Indian Ocean to Calicut; and into the history books as the 'discoverer' of the ocean route to Asia.

Mana Vikrama, the Hindu King, was ruling Calicut. He was popular across the trade world by the title '*Samoothiri Raja*' (anglicized as Zamorin of Calicut). Calicut was one of the greatest ports in the world and a cornerstone of international trade. The goods from the Far East were even shipped to Calicut first before the Arabs transported them out to Persia and Europe.

The city itself was a model of commercial prosperity and medieval importance. The city was a host to merchants and goods from every worthy trading nation in its prominent market. The people of Calicut were thriving and rich, and its ruler was strong enough to preserve his sovereignty from potent forces on the Indian peninsula.

Vasco da Gama and his men were called in an opulent court of Samoothiri Raja, as a matter of courtesy, which greatly impressed the explorers. Vasco requested for an official business discussion but they were told that there was a local custom of giving presents first to the ruler. Vasco da Gama Da Gama was very confident when he submitted "twelve pieces of striped cloth, four scarlet hoods, six hats, four strings of coral, a case of six wash-hand basins, a case of sugar, two casks of oil, and two of honey" before Samoothiri Raja. The king's men burst out into laughter at such a misery. Even the poorest Arab merchants knew that nothing less than pure gold to be presented to a king as prominent as Samoothiri Raja. Vasco was embarrassed and claimed himself to be an 'ambassador' of King of Portugal and not a mere merchant. But Samoothiri Raja was not interested in vague and lofty claims of vague ambassador of a vague King of Portugal, who offered tiny trinkets as presents to him.

Samoothiri Raja, however unimpressed, allowed Vasco da Gama to trade like other ordinary traders but no special treatment will be given to them. Vasco da Gama was not happy with the cold reception but he had no option but to comply. Vasco da Gama and his men setup a shop in Calicut, in the midst of Arab merchants who saw them as competitors, for selling goods that they brought from Europe but they realized that no one wanted them in the East. The first European trade mission was a massive failure, and when three months later Vasco da Gama's fleet departed Calicut, they left behind a particularly poor impression on the locals.

The Empires came and vanished over a long period of time, leaving their legacy and impact on India which has shaped its cultural and social structure. Indian history is vast and diverse as civilizations emerged in India followed by migrations of people for the quest of knowledge, trade and then for invasions. The countless but prominent empires like Shunga Empire, Satavahana Empire, Pallava Empire, Rashtrakuta Empire, Pala Empire, Kadamba Empire rose and perished in the span of centuries.

India has always been an oasis for the thirsty world which came to it for quenching the thirst of its wisdom, knowledge and values of the world. And this country has never disappointed and never hesitated to embrace the world with its open arms and bestowed it with infinite teachings in every sphere of human life. This great nation could not escape the clutches of Invasions. Invasion (which also means entering another country with an army as an enemy) were numerous, which India has always seen. Some of the major invasions on India can be seen in brief.

Invasion by Mahmud Ghazni

The Indian prosperity came with its own challenges of invasion and plunder in its various kingdoms by Muslim Turkish invaders which were in search of wealth for looting. These groups were barbaric and cruel and invaded parts of India with an objective of amassing wealth. They did not hesitate while killing people in order to grab their wealth. Mahmud Ghazni invaded India for the first time in 1001 A.D. and later invaded seventeen times between 1000 A.D. to 1027 A.D. Ghazni had adopted the title of But-Shikan (the destroyers of Idols) and destroyed a lot of Hindu God idols. He plundered Somnath Temple which was a rich and famous temple of India and looted Twenty Lac dinars. He was later defeated by Vijayadhara Chandela of Chandela Rajput Dynasty.

Invasion by Muhammad Ghori

In 1175 A.D., Muhammad of Ghori invaded India for plunder of wealth. Muhammad Ghori seized the fortress of Bhatinda in 1189 A.D. and then progressed into the kingdom of Prithviraj Chauhan, a great king from Chauhan Dynasty. Prithviraj Chauhan defeated Muhammad Ghori in 1191 A.D. but let go off the retreating Ghori army but recovered the fortress of Bhatinda. After a year in 1192 A.D., Ghori recovered and again invaded Prithviraj Chauhan and by using deceit, defeated Prithviraj Chauhan who was imprisoned and killed by Muhammad Ghori.

Muhammad Ghori, in 1194 A.D., invaded Jaichandra, one of the greatest Rajput rulers of Kanauj in the Battle of Chandawar, where Jaichandra was defeated and killed in the battle. Muhammad-bin-Baktiyar Khilji, one of the commanders of Muhammad of Ghori destroyed Vikramshila in 1202 A.D. and Nalanda Universities in 1203 A.D. Subsequently, Muhammad of Ghor captured Ajmer after killing several thousand defenders, enslaved many more, and destroyed the temples in the city.

Invasion by Allaudin Khilji

The invasions on India later were in a form of long-term plunders which were carried out in the name of founding kingdoms. These kingdoms were only for the exploitation of the people and extracting wealth out of them. They made no efforts of making any policies or provisions which benefitted the general people. They had an unquenchable greed for money, precious stones, silk and whatever had a value that could be grabbed and taken away. This new form of 'plunder' in the name of kingdoms was very well used by Allaudin Khilji from Khilji Dynasty. Allaudin, born in Afghanistan, was brought to India by his uncle and also his father-in-law, Jalaluddin Khilji, the king of Khilji Dynasty, who brought him up after his father's death. Allaudin killed Jalaluddin Khilji and his head was cut and fixed on a spear and paraded in his soldiers' camp. He reigned from 1296-1316 A.D. during which and also before his accession to the throne, he and his generals destroyed several Hindu temples during their military campaigns. These temples included the ones at Bhilsa (1292), Devagiri (1295), Vijapur (1298– 1310), Somnath (1299), Jhain (1301), Chidambaram (1311) and Madurai (1311). Allaudin got a huge amount of wealth, including precious metals, jewels, silk, elephants, horses, and slaves from these invasions. He killed Hindus mercilessly under his religious fanaticism and for his lust for conquest. He was however successful in resisting the Mongol invasions in India and reigned the Khilji Dynasty till his death when he was murdered.

Invasion by Mongols or Mughals

Mongol Invasions by groups from Mongolia failed in their various invading attempts on India. They were defeated by Allaudin Khilji and other Muslim sultans of Delhi Sultanate and many invasions failed. However, in 1398, Timur (also known as Tamerlane meaning 'Timur the Lame') invaded northern India and captured Delhi Sultanate. He slaughtered a hundred thousand slaves who had been captured previously in the Indian campaign out of fear that they might revolt. Timur, during his childhood, had a small band of followers with whom he raided travellers for goods, especially animals, like sheep, horses, and cattle. Timur once tried to steal a sheep from a shepherd but was shot by two arrows, one in his right leg and another in his right hand where he lost his two fingers. His injuries disabled him and stayed for his lifetime.

When Timur invaded Delhi, the Delhi Sultan Nasir-ud-Din Mahmud Shah Tughluq had war elephants armoured with chain mail and poison on their tusks. Timur's forces were afraid of the elephants so Timur had ordered his men to dig a trench in front of their position. Then camels were loaded with as much wood and hay as they could carry. When the war elephants charged, Timur set the hay on fire and poked the camels with iron sticks, causing them to charge at the elephants while they were howling in pain. Timur came to know that elephants easily panicked when the strange camels came straight at them with flames leaping from their backs. The elephants turned around and stampeded back towards their own army. Timur got an easy victory and Nasir-ud-Din Mahmud Shah Tughluq fled with his remaining forces. The capture of the Delhi Sultanate was one of Timur's biggest and most devastating victories as Delhi was one of the richest cities in the world. The city of Delhi was ransacked and reduced to ruins by Timur. Women and children were enslaved by Timur and his men.

After the fall of the city, uprisings by the local people against the Turkic-Mongols began to take place, causing a bloody massacre of those people within the city walls. Only three days later of uprising, the city stank of the decomposing bodies of people with their heads cut and being erected like pyramid structures and the bodies fed to the birds by Timur's soldiers. Timur's invasion and destruction of Delhi left caused such a destruction that it took decades for the recovery from the losses for the city.

The descendants of Timur were able to rule for years to come. Babur, his successor, caused havoc on Hindus and Sikhs in the name of religion. Thousands were massacred as the religious violence of the Muslim invaders persisted. In 1520s, the violence of Babur was witnessed by Guru Nanak, the founder of Sikhism and the first Sikh Guru, who accounted it in his four hymns. The early Mughals period of religious violence contributed to the transformation of Sikhism to militancy for self-defense. Babur's wrote his autobiography called as Baburnama, that in his campaign in northwest India, he targeted Hindus and Sikhs who were killed in an immense number, with Muslim camps building 'towers of skulls of the infidels' on hillocks. They called people of other religions who did not believe or had not converted to Islam, as 'Infidels'. Babur ordered a demolition of temple of Lord Rama which was built at the exact place of his birth. He asked his general named Mir Baqi to build Babri Masjid ("Babar's Mosque") at the same site, which was then built in 1528-1529. The re-construction of the Ram temple has been a dispute since the eighteenth century, which is resolved and a new temple of Lord Rama is built at his exact birthplace after decades' long struggle of Lord Rama's devotees.

Later came, Humayun, born in 1508, son of Babur, as a ruler of Mughal kingdom. In 1540, Humayun lost to Sher Shah Suri in the Battle of Kannauj and lost the Mughal throne to him. He later, in 1555, placed his army under the leadership of Bairam Khan, as he lacked the military skills. Bairam Khan led army defeated the armies of Sikandar Shah Suri and restored Mughal Empire in India.

Humayun's son, Akbar, who was born in 1542, came to the throne. Akbar was a typical Turkic-Mongol merciless ruler who massacred people of other faith and destroyed huge number of temples. He did not have a grand kingdom but stabilized the economy of Mughal Empire. Akbar was only fourteen years old when Humayun had died so Bairam Khan ruled on his behalf as his regent till Akbar came of age. Later, Akbar had forcibly married Salima Sultana Begum, who was the wife of his regent, Bairam Khan. Akbar's one of the motives, during his wars of aggression against various rulers, was to make their women, daughters and sisters, his slaves. Akbar's son Jahangir, his grandson Shahjahan ruled the Mughal empire and were as barbaric as their ancestors and continued to have intolerant religious policies and fought over the accession to throne leading to some expansion of Mughal empire.

The demonic Aurangzeb

Mughals emperors, who ruled the Mughal Empire, could only achieve accession to the Mughal throne by slaughtering their own brothers. The only times when they could not kill their father was due to the natural death occurring to them before the struggle for throne had begun. Remarkably, the sixth emperor of Mughal empire, son of Shahjahan, named Aurangzeb born in 1618, had all the barbarism and brutality in his veins that the former Mughal emperors had combinedly possessed. He put his father, Shahjahan, under house arrest till his death. Aurangzeb brutally killed his eldest brother Dara Sikhoh, who was to become the next king, by beheading him and getting his head presented on a tray for his inspection. He caused the death of his second eldest brother Shah Shuja by his loyal forces and killed his younger brother Murad Baksh, whom he had falsely assured that he will be the next Mughal emperor, by accusing him of murder and executing him. Aurangzeb killed his nephew, Dara Shikoh's son Sulaiman Shikoh, by poisoning him whom he had already imprisoned.

It was the cruelest emperor that Mughal empire or for that matter, any empire had ever seen. Ironically, some false accounts also describe Aurangzeb as 'Zinda Pir' (meaning 'living saint') for his 'simple living, high thinking' despite of the fact that he was the most dreadful murderer of his own brothers, nephew and had imprisoned his father and a son. Aurangzeb, a self-claimed Alamgir (meaning 'Conqueror of the world', which he was not) was the contemporary of Shivba. He was the biggest enemy of Shivba and their armies fought many battles against each other in their lives.

The times, before the birth of Shivba, were very bad for people in many parts of India. The cruel invaders were exploiting the people and making their lives miserable. These invaders had come to exploit Indian treasures and they came with a motive to grab them at any cost. The Islamic rule was being imposed on people and they were trying to build a kingdom for continued invasion and looting of India. The people were tortured and tormented by the invaders. There were forceful conversions to Islam by way of threatening and killing. The people were not allowed to follow their own religion or faith. Temples were destroyed so people could not worship or conduct rituals in them. People were fearful and had no one who could save them from the barbaric rulers. The invaders were violent and cunning and appeared like hungry demons that set their feet in India only to cast a curse on this holy and prosperous land.

It could be attributed to the holy land of good deeds of this country and its good fortune that it could be rescued eventually every time from one disaster to another, appearing in the guise of invaders who came and wreaked havoc on the people. It was time that the saviour would be born to rise up for righteousness and end the indiscriminate butchery of men and women across the Bharatvarsh that is India. People prayed for their lives, their dignity and wished that the darkness in their lives would be warded off by the Rise of the Sun which would light up their worlds, forever.

Birth of Son of the Soil

Shivaji Maharaj, a virtuous king, a brave warrior, an ideal and obedient son, lived in seventeenth century India. Jijabai, his mother and father Shahaji Raje, a commander, were his proud parents.

He was born on 19th February 1630 A.D. on a fort called Shivneri, near Pune, Maharashtra State in India. This was very good news for the villagers around Fort Shivneri and they rejoiced that Jijabai and Shahaji Raje is blessed with a child. This child happened to be a blessing for millions later in his illustrious life as a king. Jijabai named her son 'Shivaji' after Goddess Shivai.

Jijabai once had a dream before she was to conceive a baby. She saw a baby sitting in her lap. The baby was dusky with lovely sparkling eyes. He had four hands, each holding a lotus flower, mace, conch shell and a chakra (wheel). He had a white beads garland around his neck and had a smiling face. He had an aura of happiness and bliss around him which she could feel. It was Lord Vishnu whom she saw in her dream!

Jijabai, soon after she conceived, felt an unusual heaviness in her body. She had strange cravings while she was pregnant like wanting to ride on elephants and climbing forts. She craved to fight a battle wielding a sword in her hands and shoot arrows from a bow and gain victories. She felt like sitting on a throne only to protect the poor people. She felt like she wants to capture forts to establish a good rule and making charities for the benefit of people. This is a hero what her baby was manifesting into.

Shivaji Maharaj was born after sunset. There was a celebration in every house at Shivneri. The fort was decorated with flowers, beautiful garlands were put on the doors of the fort, sweets were distributed to the villagers and everyone was excited to see the baby of Jijabai and Shahaji Raje. The baby was so lovely, adorable and cute that villagers instantly fell in love with him. The baby was healthy that grew into a joyful child whom they, later, fondly called 'Shivba'.

3. JIJABAI, THE FIRST TEACHER

Jijabai, a brave and ambitious lady, knew that Shivba was a child blessed with exceptional brilliance, vigour and strength. She was no ordinary lady herself. She had vowed to raise her son to be become a saviour to countless suffering people in those times. The invaders came to India and had made their kingdoms and were troubling the poor and innocent people. Jijabai knew that her son would grow up to build a kingdom for the people and protect them from cruel enemies.

The political power in Maharashtra was dominated by Maratha families, one of which Shivba was born in. The Maratha caste generally composed of ninety-six or 96 clans, originally formed in the earlier centuries from the amalgamation of families from the various castes in Maharashtra. Many of the clans took to military service in the sixteenth century for the Deccan sultanates or the Mughals and majority of them were farmers. Since these clans were valiant warriors and had strong muscular built, they were preferred for military services. It was their willingness to take up daredevilish and arduous tasks due to being generally strong-willed added to their profile.

It is said and written by many authors, poets or sometimes by historians about the Sisodia Rajput ancestry of Bhonsales. But this claim has not found any backing by the historical evidences. Many noted historians have refuted this claim and stated that there was no such ancestry of Bhonsales. Gaga Bhatt and Balaji Auji Chitnis claimed to have found Shivba's genealogy showing that he was a descendant of Sisodias and therefore a Kshatriya. This does not shed sufficient light on the ancestry of Shivba or his contribution to such findings. There may have been an attempt by Gaga Bhatt to do a validation exercise in absence of which none of the other Brahmins and priests would have approved of it and identified the coronation as a legit one. Shivba has never called himself a Rajput even before the claim of Gaga Bhatt, which he never needed to. Every Rajput, if the meaning is to be constrained to a generational offsprings from a king, the ones at the outset of it, may have risen in ranks or declared themselves as head of community or group. So, the Rajput tag was not necessary if it was not for the closed and monopolized group of priests who could, only by the faith and belief, conduct the ritual of coronation.

Jijabai was a daughter of Lakhoji Jadhav, a Maratha commander. Maratha generally refers to the people who spoke Marathi language. He also had four sons.

Lakhoji Jadhav was a commander of forces for Nizamshah and known as a courageous and righteous man. He was a popular and respected person among the locals of Sindkhed Raja where he had his estates. He was one of the Maratha Sardars ("chiefs") who commanded a lot of respect from the soldiers. It was common that many such Maratha Sardars were in the service of Sultanates like Nizamshah, Qutub Shah, Baritshah, Adil Shah, Mughal, Barid Shah. Lakhoji Jadhav was loyal to Nizamshah and held the position of a Sardar.

Shivba belonged to Bhonsale family and his grandfather Maloji Bhonsale started out as a chieftain in Verul village. Lakhoji Jadhav had four sons who were in the service of Nizamshah. Maloji Bhosale was of the opinion that his son Shahaji Raje was an eligible bachelor and Jijabai would be a perfect suit for being his bride. But this idea was rejected by Lakhoji as he was a Sardar and Maloji was a Shiledar whose rank was lower to his. But Maloji was no ordinary person and possessed skills worthy of an able commander. His son Shahaji was a brave young courageous man with no parallel. He was rising in ranks and earned a reputation of being a skilled and strategic leader.

Maloji, once, while tilling their fields with his brother Vithoji, came across a ferocious snake. Snakes, in many folklores, are believed to protect the treasures and such a sign was enough for Maloji to believe that there could be a hidden treasure in the fields. The folklore may or may not be true but Maloji tried his luck and dug out places in the field. In unusual chance of luck, Maloji found seven pots of gold coins in his field hidden mysteriously. This was a great fortune which led to turning the life of Maloji and his descendants. Maloji and Vithoji were able to buy arms, horses, saddles, tents, cattles and keep army troops at their disposal and then enter into the services of Nizamshah. Malojirao also spent a huge portion of his new found wealth in the construction of many temples, giving alms to the poors, and also for excavating a large tank on the arid Shambhu Mahadev hill in the Satara district. Malojirao reconstructed the famous temple Grishneshwar near Verul (Ellora) in Maharashtra. This brought him a lot of praise from the pilgrims who came to this holy place in large numbers. Maloji's rank was raised although he had a small army but that was enough to get an opportunity to prove his worth. Nizamshah was aware that Maloji, Vithoji and their sons were very useful in his army. So, he insisted Lakhoji to marry off his daughter to Maloji's son Shahaji to which Lakhoji reluctantly agreed.

Bhonsale family had grown in stature. After Maloji's and subsequently Vithoji's death, Shahaji Raje became the commander the army raised by them.

There were later, for some reasons, a friction between Lakhoji and Shahaji Raje. The Maratha sardars were once attending a Darbar (court session) of the Nizamshah and while they were departing the palace, the elephant of a sardar named Khandagale became unruly and trampled some pedestrians to death. Dattaji, son of Jadhavrao, attacked the elephant, and a skirmish began between him and Khandagale, who was assisted by the sons of Vithoji. A fight ensued between Dattaji (son of Lakhoji Jadhavrao) and Sambhaji (son of Vithoji Bhonsale and cousin of Shahaji Raje) in which Dattaji was killed. Lakhoji Jadhavrao, who had already departed, heard the shocking news of his son's death and returned infuriated, to attack Sambhaji. Shahaji arrived to help his cousin Sambhaji but the battle ensued in which Sambhaji was killed. This incidence resulted in enmity between the Bhonsales and Jadhavs.

Lakhoji Jadhavrao camp was in the pursuit of Shahaji Raje to seek revenge so Shahaji had to keep out the pregnant Jijabai from the perils of the combat. In the meanwhile, Lakhoji left the services of Nizamshah for a brief period to join Mughals due to chaos caused with Nizamshahi. Lakhoji rejoined Nizamshah court after a while where he had been working along with his sons. Upon his return in 1629, Lakhoji along with his three sons, except one named Bahadurji, went to pay humble homage to the Nizamshah, who was still disenchanted with Jadhavrao. Nizamshah, in the feat of fury, murdered the loyal Lakhoji Jadhavrao and his three sons in the open court of Nizamshahi. This was a a devastating blow to the Jadhav family where Jijabai lost her family to the tyrant ruler like Nizamshah. Shahaji left Nizamshahi services as he was angry at the murders of his father-in-law and his sons.

Shahaji Raje kept Jijabai carrying the child at Fort Shivneri under the supervision of his cousin Vishwasrao who was commanding the fort. After the Jadhav camp was wiped out by Nizamshah, it was Nizamshahi forces which were seeking Shahaji Raje which made him take refuge for Jijabai at Shivneri Fort.

Jijabai was witnessing the turn of events where her father, three brothers were murdered in broad daylight and her husband was fighting Nizamshahi forces being on run while she was carrying Shivba in her womb. She was a fiercely brave lady who stood firmly against all the odds in the face of severe adversity, pain and grief. Her anger, grief, and emotions like ignited flames churned into her womb to cast the being of her child, who later became as fiercely driven by the will of independence, as his mother.

Those times were full of challenges for Shivba and his people. There were cruel rulers like Adilshah, Nizamshah and Mughals who were troubling people and looting their crops and money and even brutally killed large number of people. Shivba despised this and it made him very furious even as a small child. He showed early signs of leadership and his unwavering affection for the people who were harassed by the cruel rulers. He cared for the welfare of the people which was not common for the rulers. The rulers used to extract the commoners of their money, crops and valuables under the guise of taxes levied upon them for ruling them. The policies of these rulers were discriminative and unfair as all they wanted was to extract as much from people as they could. Rulers, who were infact foreign invaders, did not care about the people.

Shivba as he grew cared for his people like they were his own siblings. He was fond of people around him and created an aura such that everyone liked to be around him. He was a natural when it came to attracting everyone towards him and his charisma grew with him.

Shivba borrowed a lot from Jijabai when it came to determination and courage in the face of adversity. Jijabai herself had faced the untimely deaths of her family members, conflicts that affected her life which she was not a part of. She had experienced the pains of brutal killing of her father and brothers and knew that no matter how loyal anyone was to these Sultanates, all they got in return was deceit and derogation. Her father was a loyal Sardar all his life, and despite of being a capable commander and could form his own army to fight against the Deccan Sultanates, he chose to remain in the loyal service all his life. Her brothers were young and not at any fault that they had to face the death in this merciless massacre. She was agonized by this personal pain and had no respite from the struggle during her pregnancy. It was gruesome to carry a child in her womb while being fearful of its fate.

Jijabai and Shahaji Raje knew that although Jijabai and their unborn child were under the watch of Vishwasrao, they could be attacked at Shivneri and that would end their hopes forever. Shahaji Raje was under constant attacks from the foes which he tackled as an accomplished warrior but it kept him on the run as he could not stay at one place for long. Jijabai obviously could not have joined Shahaji Raje in this delicate condition although she was a lady who would fiercely stand for her husband in adversity. She was on Shahaji Raje's side even when her father got into a conflict with Shahaji Raje in some unfortunate turn of events. But Jijabai is not any other women who would be torn down by hardship and misfortune. And this is what Shivba saw in her mother while he was in her womb.

Shivba did not only learn being resilient but also applied it in his later life. If Shivba did not have a mother like Jijabai, he would not have been as great a king as he was. Jijabai put her heart and soul in shaping her child into a mighty saviour of helpless and downtrodden people. Shivba was a powerful manifestation of her strong will and resolute.

Jijabai told Shivba a lot of stories about the Kings, warriors and saints. He used to love listening to his mother's stories. Jijabai told Shivba the historic epics like Ramayana, Mahabharata and lessons from Bhagawat Gita. Shahaji Raje had appointed a Purohit or a teacher for Shivba to teach and recite Ramayana and understand Mahabharata. Shivba heard stories of Krishna, Ganesha and other Hindu gods and goddesses. Jijabai also taught Shivba about Tukaram, Dnyaneshwar, and Namdev Maharaj who were great saints. Shivba was told about Vedas, Upanishads and Puranas, which were books of great knowledge and moral values. Hindu scriptures are a treasure of knowledge and there is nothing in the world which is not in these scriptures. Ramayana taught Shivba the moral code which Lord Rama abided himself to, value of relationships, virtues of a king; Mahabharata taught him the good and bad deeds, consequences of one's actions, fighting for Dharma; Bhagawat Gita taught the unwavering devotion in the supreme God who indeed rules the world and the values of life and eternal truth.

Shivba was a devout Hindu and great devotee of Goddess Tulja Bhavani. He worshipped the Goddess every day and derived his strength from his devotion towards Tulja Bhavani. Bhavani is a form of Goddess Parvati who is worshipped in present day Maharashtra, Gujarat, Rajasthan, Telangana, Northern Karnataka, and Nepal. Bhavani literally means 'giver of life', the power of nature, the source of creative energy. The famous temple of Goddess Tulja Bhavani was located at Tuljapur located in present day Dharashiv District in Maharashtra. Shivba, as a king, used to visit this temple to worship the Goddess but later when Swarajya grew and he could visit frequently, he built a temple for the Goddess at Pratapgad for his worship.

Shivba was taught the history of our great nation so he could learn how this country came into being. At a very young age, Shivba understood what others his age could not. He was undoubtedly a brilliant child who had a great vision for himself. The reason why Shivba was ahead of his time was Jijabai, who taught him to envision the independence while others were drowned in slavery. The independence at that time was from the cruel rulers of Sultanates. And to achieve the independence, Shivba needed a kingdom which was established for the welfare of people. Jijabai called it 'Swarajya' which meant 'self-governance or self-rule'.

A new kingdom of Swarajya was meant to emerge for the people's rule where they found freedom and dignity. But this thought was a very distant and a blur dream at that time when Sultanates were crushing the people for their greed. Shahaji Raje was aware that Islamic invaders wanted to suppress every effort at the formation of a Hindu kingdom as they knew that India had such kingdoms earlier and any such kingdom could wipe out their existence. They made a deliberate effort to curb the traces of such kingdoms which could inspire people into putting up a revolt against the Sultanates. The religious autonomy had completely vanished and there was a threat of existence to the Hindu religion. People were made to convert by coercion and those who refused met the consequence of losing their lives. The invaders, however, could not convert everyone as there was a resistance from some sections of people. It was easier for the Islamic invaders to keep some Hindu population at their disposal so they could utilize them for being their slaves, serve in army and sometimes to suppress the possible revolt. There were kingdoms in India which posed serious threat to these brutal rulers but, eventually with time, these kingdoms perished.

There were a few brave Maratha warriors who aspired for the independence from the burning hell in which they were living. But their aspirations could not take shape and it remained as mere dreams. Shahaji Raje was one of such leaders who wanted to cause a transformation of their zamindari or land bearing into a kingdom of their own. Shivba was about to create a new kingdom which would set free millions from the clutches of the Islamic rulers' brutality. Shahaji Raje saw that his son was not an ordinary child and had exceptional skills to be a king. He thought that this dream could see daylight if Shivba could be a king someday so arranged for a few ministers and money so that Shivba could do what he deeply aspired. There were a few forts at Shahaji Raje's disposal so he let

Shivba take over and form an army of men which could fight for their common cause - Independence.

Not everyone subscribed to this idea of Swarajya. Many Maratha sardars were against this, some who did not want to 'betray' their Muslim masters, and some who had their share of animosity with Shahaji Raje, so they did not support this huge undertaking of Shahaji Raje. Even after Shivba grew up to be a king, this internal resistance never stopped, for instance, A sardar of Adil Shah, Chandrarao More from Javali, near Mahabaleshwar, bitterly wrote to Shivba that who made him a king and claimed that he was the real king. He fought a battle with Shivba and was defeated so he ran away to hide in the mountain of Rairi. Some Sardars never joined the Swarajya, some remained under doubt on its fate and some even questioned it. This later became a reason why coronation where Shivba became a king with a title of 'Chhatrapati' was needed.

Shivba was lucky to find brave and courageous men on his side while he took on the mammoth task of building Swarajya. And that was enough for Shivba to have these men and invaluable guidance of Jijabai. Some kings probably never had the feat of victory as they never had a mother like Jijabai who was the foundation of Shivba's dreams that came true. She was not just a watchful mother but also a great political and strategic advisor to Shivba. She was a teacher that none other had; she was a friend which never let Shivba alone. It would be fair to say that it was a great fortune of Shivba to have a mother, as determined and strong-willed as Jijabai.

Jijabai, with the support of Shahaji Raje though in his absentia, got Shivba trained in many skills. He could read and write early while learning Marathi, Sanskrit, Hindi, Farsi (Persian), Urdu, Konkani, Kannada, Braj and some others while he picked after growing up. There was a poet called Jayram Pinde who called Shahaji Raje as '*Dwadashbhasha Lalit Shahanareshwar*' which meant that he was an expert in twelve languages. Shivba, following the footsteps of his father, was conversant with many languages that were needed by a commander in those times. Shivba was taught Swordsmanship, Archery, Javelin, and martial techniques used for combats. He was taught Sanskrit by a pandit who was specially summoned by Jijabai. She knew that she is not raising just a child but a virtuous king who would lead the people out of darkness. Shivba was a quick learner and surprised Jijabai by his sharp intellect. He asked questions out of his curiosity and was eager to learn more than he was taught by his Gurus.

Jijabai, or Aausaheb, as Shivba used to call her, like any mother of a child, was the first teacher of Shivba. But Jijabai was beyond a mother. She kindled in him a sense of independence and justice that transformed the lives of millions. She has had a lasting impact on history of this nation. It would certainly not have been the same. Jijabai was a true Guru to Shivba who shaped the life of its disciple which later shaped the Indian history. Jijabai's motherly shelter over Shivba, fortunately, remained for a very long time in his life. Shivba could not spend a lot of years together with his father Shahaji Raje but her mother was always by his side, till he had become a 'Chhatrapati'. Jijabai saw her son summit the highest peak of accomplishment by being a Chhatrapati ('Emperor') of a new kingdom called Swarajya and then she left for her heavenly abode on eleventh day after Shivba's coronation ceremony.

There would, without an iota of doubt, be no sons like Shivba, if there are no mothers like Jijabai. Any nation, which wants a virtuous and mighty king or a leader to be their saviour, would first have to see if their daughters are raised well, treated well and instilled with values of morality, justice, faith and righteousness. The hands that rock the cradle, rule the world is said truly and it has been true with Shivba who ruled his kingdom and expanded it by leaps and bounds. He laid a foundation of an empire which later went ahead to conquer parts of the Indian sub-continent from Attock (Afghanistan) to Tanjavur (Tamilnadu).

4. YOUNG SHIVBA AND HIS PLAY

Shivba was no ordinary being and it was clear right from his childhood. The small feet knew no bounds. He had the curiosity to learn new things that came his way. Shivba was brilliant in his learning and as a fast learner; he wanted to grasp everything in his mind. He picked up tips and tricks from his village friends as they often went in the jungle to play.

The times were not safe for Jijabai and his young son. Shahaji was in Bijapur and out of the bounds of Mughal sardars so they started the hunt for Jijabai and her son. Jijabai was under the constant fear for Shivba as the enemies of Shahaji Raje were on a prowl to capture them. No matter how fearless Jijabai was, a mere thought of Shivba getting captured by these brutal rulers made her anxious. As she knew that although, if captured, she could only serve as a captive, but Shivba would be in too much danger as the enemies would even kill him for their revenge against Shahaji Raje. It was essential to keep Shivba away and safe from these invaders till he grows up. Jijabai, a lone woman, with her husband being far away, faced the difficulties all on her own. It was disastrous and she was surrounded by inevitable darkness but she created light for Shivba and herself by her courage and deeds. She not only kept Shivba safe but also made him a fearlessly independent, morally awakened and ambitious child.

Shivba's initial years as a child were spent at Shivneri fort. His forefathers had been zamindars in the regions close to Pune. Shahaji Raje had the local affiliation and people looked upto him as an honest and trustworthy Maratha Sardar who would not let bring any harm to his people. The fact that there was no Maratha kingdom then, people had to rely on the Sardar to protect their own jagirs. But it did not stop the Deccan Sultanates from exploiting the people and looting them of their possessions.

Jijabai did not want her son to be another Sardar in the service of Deccan or Delhi Sultanates. Although her husband Shahaji Raje was an accomplished and respected Sardar, she knew that it was ultimately the Shahs of these Sultanates who ruled the kingdoms and decided the fates of their people. She wanted Shivba to establish Swarajya which was a dream too large to be realistic in those circumstances. Jijabai did not only give birth to Shivba but also gave birth to the dream of Swarajya.

Shivba was a joyful child who stayed around his mother all day. But it was not his mother alone who took care of Shivba. Jijabai had a few female helpers or Midwives around her to look after her household. The epicenter of her world, like any other mother, was her child Shivba. Shahaji Raje was away at the battle with Daryakhan Pathan near Sahyadri foothills when Shivba was born.

Jijabai was mesmerized by the birth of her child, who was the fruit of her devotion and answered prayer by Goddess Shivai. She knew that she had been blessed. Jijabai was in her splendid yellow saree with beautiful ornaments and baby Shivba in her lap as the rituals were carried out after the birth of Shivba. Jijabai had envisioned her child to be greatest king, a saviour who would spread the bounds of his rule in all directions, lead a virtuous kingdom, eliminate the shackles of slavery of the people and lead them under a unified rule of the pious Swarajya.

On the twelfth day of the birth, an auspicious ritual of blessing the newborn is carried out which is called as Barse (in Marathi, also known as 'Naming Ceremony'). On Shivba's naming ceremony, he was worn a small crown-like headwear endowed with jewels and pearls. Shivba also had diamond and red jewels on his armbands wrapped around his small arms. He was wearing a black beaded neck chain around his baby neck. He had magnificent bracelets around his wrist and baby anklets on his baby feet. The baby was taken in the tender Sun as a part of worship in the ritual. All the rituals were graciously followed for the baby Shivba in the ceremony where he was named officially as 'Shivaji'.

Shahaji Raje returned from the battle where he defeated the arrogant Daryakhan Pathan and reached Shivneri to see his newborn son for the first time. He was ecstatic to see the child and took Shivba in his arms with great delight. Shahaji Raje ordered to distribute gems, cows, horses and elephants, gold coins among his people out of his sheer happiness and as a charity on this auspicious occasion.

Shivba was growing as an adorable baby. He was a jolly child who lit up his surroundings with his baby cheers. The only time that he would cry was when he was hungry and needed to feed. As he grew older and could crawl, he became more playful. He could see his own reflection on the shining floor while crawling on his small knees and would try to quickly catch the reflection. Shivba being a fast crawler would often race with his own reflection to get ahead of it. His baby feet sole was so tender red in colour which would reflect in the crystals worn on him while he crawled around the Waada (traditional house) on the fort. This reflection in the crystals would make the crystals look like spectacular ruby gems on baby Shivba.

Shivba baby would play and crawl in the Waada and get the dust all over him. Jijabai could hear the sound of the clinking gems on his anklets all day which engrossed her deeply. Shivba would play in the garden and would eat the tender soil when Jijabai is not around. Jijabai would however find out as every mother does when their child is at play. Shivba was curious and he was very active child. It was tough to keep a tab on this little baby who was exploring the world around him.

Traditionally, Waadas had high doorstep (Umbartha or threshold) at the main entrance. Shivba found it difficult to cross the doorstep with his tiny feet. There was a nanny or *daai* to help Jijabai take care of Shivba while he was just a baby. Shivba would want to do things by crawling around the house and would take the help of nanny to get up where he couldn't do himself being too small.

Shivba would see the reflection of Sun in the house and would cry so his mother would get it for him. This used to amuse Jijabai and make her laugh at the innocence of the baby. Shivba's had started developing deciduous teeth and had small white teeth growing from his gums. Shivba would play around the Waada and his nannies would chase him. He used to play in dust and throw the dirt on himself just like how playfully the newly teething elephant does. The nanny who would chase him to discipline him would be astonished by the baby's play.

Nanny would take Shivba to play and engage him with many tricks. She used to clap to amuse Shivba who would laugh and dance by making his babyish gestures. He would learn new words from the nanny. When Shivba would be happy, he would take out the jewellery worn by him and give it to his nannies.

Shivba had many elephants and horses kept by Shahaji Raje at his disposal and could get any of them to entertain him but he would still play with his small clay elephants and horses. Shivba had long hair as a toddler which made him look adorable. He used to run behind the peacocks so that he can get peacock feathers to play with.

Shivba, as he grew older, could imitate sounds of parrot, peacock and cuckoo so immaculately that they felt real. Shivba learnt to imitate other birds and animals as well. He would come closer and scare his nanny by making the sound of Tiger's roar. It also came very naturally to Shivba, as a child, to imitate the sounds which he heard around him. He would express his happiness by running around in circles in the Waada and make neighing sounds like a horse. Shivba would make loud trumpets sounds of elephant when he was excited and play with his nannies and friends.

Shivba was very playful and a naughty child who

was also deeply engaged with people around him. He kept his friends around him and took them along in his every childish adventure. He had his impactful presence in the Waada and every place that he went to, filled it with his aura. Shivba's ventures kept everyone engrossed and it was him who kept the places lively. It was easy to guess for everyone when Shivba would be around them; such was his presence and influence, even as a child.

The most noteworthy game that Shivba played as a child was making castle on a hilltop with stones and mud and claiming it as his own 'Fort'. This little childish game remained relevant, later on a greater scale, for Shivba in his lifetime as he constructed and captured around four hundred forts. He was later considered an expert on forts and referred to as Gadpati (pundit or expert of forts) as he had impeccable understanding of Fort building. Shivba was very fond of forts as a child, the fondness which he inherited from Jijabai. Jijabai and Shahaji Raje were aware that the forts are the backbone of any kingdom. Shivba truly loved the forts he made as a child as well as those he made or captured once he grew as a king. The small mud and stone forts which he made showed his inclination, and subsequently resolve, as a child towards building a kingdom for the people. This small game of children helped Shivba in knowing how vital forts were for fulfilling his dream of Swarajya and which later culminated into building of such forts which stand tall and proud even on the present day.

The toddler, the playful Shivba had many games to play with his friends, one of which was Blind man's Buff, a game in which one player is blindfolded and he tries to touch other player without being able to see them. Shivba would hide in a corner of Waada so he would not get caught but his friends would find him and that would make Shivba burst into laughter. Shivba would play with ball and whenever it fell down from his little hands, he would hit the bouncing ball down so it would not bounce again. He would throw the ball high up in the air to catch it keeping his face and hands up watching the ball fall down and pose as if he was dancing at that moment on his tiny feet. Shivba would love to spin the wooden spin-top like most children do. He had a lot of games to play and he would play the whole day.

Shivba was also a naughty and adorable child which made him everyone's favourite. Nannies would try to show their finger in order to scold the young Shivba but that did not stop him from playing his small mischiefs. Shivba would sometimes not listen to Nannies when they asked to eat food or drink water. They would have to get hold of small Shivba to make him sleep but he would still not sleep and did as he liked. Shivba would playfully run away when Jijabai would call him while playing with his friends. But then he would come to his mother when he would be hungry and sleepy. Jijabai would then light the household oil lamps and then read him stories of Rama, Krishna and other stories of saints and pious persons. She told him stories of brave men which inspired him to be courageous. The devotional songs of great Saints like Namdeo, Eknath and Dnyaneshwar were instilled in Shivba, immense faith in Hindu religion, respect for saints and admiration for brave men. Jijabai taught Shivba to read and write different languages.

Shivba soon learnt to imitate sounds of other birds, animals and understood how the forest dwellers lived. Forests were closer and important part of the lives of people then. Forests were very dense and greener than what they are today. They got wood for fire and fruits with other essentials from the forest itself. Shivba would visit the huts of his friends and eat the simple meal they offered. It was usually onion and Bhakri (locally popular round flatbread). Village kids showed Shivba how they lived and it was because of this, Shivba had a greater understanding of local people and their issues. Shivba was deeply affectionate towards his people and in return these people would do anything for Shivba. They never ceased supporting Shivba in his great task of Swarajya.

Shivba lived, ate, drank and slept among his poor but loyal friends and they later became his biggest strength. The children of Mavalas or the soldiers could climb the trees like monkeys and imitate sounds like birds. They adapted to their surroundings and learnt to survive the forests. Shivba learnt all this from the children who lived near Shivneri. Shivba's bravery came from his exceptional parents but the survival skills, that would take him a long way, came from these children, who were his friends.

5. SHIVBA AND HIS STORIES

Little Shivba had a strong role model in his own mother who stood against all the odds and faced the adversity with grace. She was a daughter of Lakhoji Jadhav, a brave and accomplished Sardar who raised her by instilling in her a sense of pride and dignity. No matter how worse the circumstances grew, Jijabai held her ground and turned the adversity into great prosperity. Shivba witnessed her resilience right from his birth when there was such unrest that she had to move from one place to another to save their lives. The situation became a little better when Shahaji Raje kept pregnant Jijabai at Shivneri but they knew enemies were on a prowl.

As Shivba grew, he understood that Jijabai was not only brave woman but also an intelligent woman. Jijabai handled administrative and political matters with exceptional flair. His mother was a living legend for Shivba from where he learnt leadership and governance. The most noteworthy inheritance of Shivba from his mother, apart from courage and leadership, was a deep and profound sense of justice.

Shivba was a happy child who was very active and liked to make friends. He would like to strike a conversation with anyone whom he met out of his natural curiosity. He never hesitated to ask questions to anyone and was generally outgoing and expressive of his thoughts. He was a very confident child and did not reserve his thoughts on what he strongly felt about. Shivba was very adaptive and mixed well with his friends who hailed from poor or middle-class families.

Shivba was a fair person and he instinctively treated people with equal terms irrespective of them being a Zamindar (landlord) or a peasant. He did not care about the person's religion, caste, or class and treated everyone with his deep and natural affection he had for people. Shivba was immensely generous right from his childhood. He liked to share what he had, with everyone around him.

Shivba came from a very affluent and respected family and he had everything he needed at his disposal. It was not very common to own horses, elephants, huge palace and own thousands of hectares of land even for Sardars. Shahaji Raje had everything that Shivba needed to lead an ultra-luxurious life and spent his life into riches. Shahaji Raje had enough wealth that Shivba would not have to do any work in his entire life. Furthermore, if Shivba wanted, Shahaji Raje could have made him a Sardar in the court of any Sultanate using his good reputation and Shivba would have led a comfortable and lavish life sitting in a palace full of extravagance, leisure, and opulence. But this is Shivba; a blessed child, a saviour, son of the motherland, who rejected all the luxuries and riches, just for the independence of his motherland and freedom of his people.

Most Marathas in those times were farmers, some called themselves Kunbi and agricultural produce was their primary source of livelihood. As the Delhi and Deccan Sultanates flourished, they needed men of valour to fight and perish for them. Marathas were perfect for the job given their loyalty and devotion towards their masters in those times. The people in Maharashtra mainly relied on agriculture but that could barely take care of their subsistence. So, they used their military skills and courage to find work in the armies of the Sultanates who could pay them well. But this would lead to drain of superbly capable commanders to these Sultanates where they died for the Sultans who were oppressive and cruel to people. Many Maratha Sardars knew this but they were left with not much choice.

Shahaji Raje despite of being an exceptional Sardar who had large number of soldiers to his command, found it difficult to establish the kingdom for people. The attempt at forming a kingdom was met with dire consequences of battles fought with combined formidable forces of Sultanates. The Deccan sultanates and Delhi Sultanate or Mughals peculiarly came together to fight a Hindu kingdom which was commonly seen by them as a threat. In other times, they were ready to shed each other's blood for the thirst of conquest. This trait was known to Shivba and he detested Sultanates as they were very exploitative and greedy.

Shivba knew that Maratha sardars are capable of strong pillars of Swarajya and wanted to keep them together if he had to build a kingdom. It was unusual for such a young child to have known such political and social situations at such depths. Shivba's morality was extremely high and the history speaks of his moral conduct in many ways such as *Bakhar* (prosaic narrative), biographies, stories, poetry, *Powada* (traditional ballads). Such manifestations describe Shivba and his glory as a king and give us a glimpse of what our Shivba and his times looked like.

Shivba was a quick learner. He had learnt a lot of life lessons right from his childhood which deeply impacted him and infact prepared him for his glorious life as a king.

There are some stories of Shivba as a child, written in many historical accounts and told over generations which serve as a source of details on how Shivba may have been in his early days.

Stolen Flowers

Jijabai had a small but a beautiful garden at their Waada. Once there were many flowers which bloomed in the garden. There was a boy from the neighbourhood, who would raid the garden and pluck and steal the flowers. Shivba noticed this act of the boy but did not scold him. He instead planted a new sapling in his courtyard, which was a clever way to teaching a lesson.

The sapling started growing into a small plant. The boy learnt a lesson about the value of hard-work and patience and he never came to Shivba's garden to steal flowers ever again.

Encounter with the Tiger cub

Shivba used to play in the forests with his friends, who knew the forests too well. One fine day, when Shivba was strolling the forest, he encountered a tiger cub. Tiger cub is accompanied by the Tigress so it is not a very good idea to be anywhere near the cub. Shivba, the brave boy, was not scared of the Tigress. He went near the cub and started petting it. The cub played with Shivba as if it were tamed. His friends were really afraid of this daredevilish gesture. Shivba let the cub be on his own and left the forest. Shivba showed his early signs of bravery and became a fearless warrior.

Mahanaayak

Shivba and his friends entertained themselves by playing their little games around the Waada. They sometimes ventured into the forests for their adventures. They also watched the plays for their entertainment. Once Shivba went to watch a performance of a play called 'Mahanaayak' which depicted the story of a brave and just king. Shivba was deeply influenced by the portrayal of the king and aspired to be one when he grows up. The little folklores and legends of great kings added up to the Shivba's aspiration to build Swarajya for the people. Shivba was preparing to be a great king and he was inspired enough to be one.

Curious Shivba

Shivba had a quenchless curiosity about the world around him. He would accompany his mother on walks and ask her a lot of questions about plants, animals, people and everything surrounding them. His curiosity was not limited to the books but also in learning from observing and interacting with his environment.

Shivba had a keen interest in various subjects, including literature and military strategy. Despite his young age, Shivba asked insightful questions and involved in intelligent conversations with elders. His ability to grasp complex concepts and the depth of his understanding at such a young age was notable.

Even as a small child, Shivba displayed strategic and brilliant thinking. He was particularly fond of the game 'Ashtapada,' an ancient Indian board game, similar to chess. Shivba not only played to win but also studied his opponents' moves and predicted the tactics played so it enriched his learning from each game. Shivba's early interest in strategy games was a clear indication of his future military acumen as a king.

Shivba received training in his military skills from a tender age. He learned horse riding, archery, and swordsmanship, perfecting his skills as a warrior. Shivba's training under the supervision of teachers and military experts prepared him for his future campaigns and made him a great warrior.

The Boiling Pot Incident

Shivba was once chased by his pursuers so he sought refuge in a local woman's house. Shivba was concealing his true identity. The smart woman decided to test him. So, she asked Shivba to stir a boiling pot of lentils. The woman thought she would come to know if he was a commoner by this boiling pot test. The royal or affluent child would not know how to stir a boiling pot. But Shivba, a brilliant child that he was, not only calmly stirred the pot but also tasted the lentils to check if it was cooked well. Shivba showed his courage and presence of mind in such a situation which impressed the woman so she helped him escape from his pursuers.

The Farmer's Complaint

Shivba was a smart child. He was aware of what went on in his surroundings. He deeply cared for his people and knew what they needed. He also tried to find out the problems his problem faced. Once, when Shivba was ten years old, he overheard a farmer complaining about the injustice of high taxes imposed by local officials. Shivba was curious and concerned, so he went asked the farmer for details. People would share their concerns with Shivba, such was his persona. After understanding the issue, he went to his father, Shahaji Raje who was the actual ruler of the region and discussed the matter. Shivba brought respite to the farmers by getting the high taxes removed by taking this to his father. Shahaji Raje was happy with Shivba's concern for farmers and felt really proud of this young boy. This showcased Shivba's early awareness of social issues and administrative affairs.

The Mango Incident

Shivba was a witty child. He knew how to turn a difficult situation into a desirable one. Once, when Shivba was a young boy, he visited the orchards which were known for their delicious mangoes. Shivba being very fond of mangoes couldn't resist the temptation as a child and decided to pluck a few mangoes for himself.

His teacher who accompanied him caught Shivba in the act and reprimanded him for stealing mangoes from his orchard. The teacher questioned Shivba about why he stole the mangoes. Shivba was very calm and he cleverly replied that he didn't steal them but had just borrowed the mangoes to taste them. He further explained that he intended to plant the mango seeds and grow more trees, so in the future, there would be an abundance of mangoes for everyone.

Shivba was a small child but impressed the teacher by his response. The teacher recognized Shivba's intelligence and foresight. This was an early sign of Shivba's strategic thinking and turning an adverse situation into a favourable one.

Tricky Test of Loyalty

Shivba, once in his teens, visited the house of a local feudal lord named Mulla Ibrahim, on the insistence of his father Shahaji Raje. Shivba was very young and he had not yet established his kingdom. Mulla Ibrahim, who was loyal to the Adil Shah, the ruler of Bijapur, decided to test Shivba's loyalty towards Adil Shah. The feudal lord was cunning and wanted to test the loyalty of free spirited Shivba towards Adil Shah. Shivba had never pledged loyalty to those who exploited his people.

During Shivba's visit, the feudal lord Mulla Ibrahim placed a pot of hot oil in the courtyard of his house. Mulla pretended that it was a customary bath offering and told Shivba that it was a tradition for guests to dip their hands into the boiling oil as a mark of respect.

Shivba, instead of reacting with fear or submission, calmly and confidently walked towards the pot. He approached the pot and then nonchalantly dipped his fingers into the supposedly boiling oil and then rubbed his wet fingers on his head as if it were a sacred anointment.

Mulla Ibrahim, witnessing this fearless act, was both astonished and impressed with Shivba's bravery and quick thinking. He not only won him the admiration of those present at the courtyard, but also sent a strong demonstration about his strong will and determination.

While the historical accuracy of these stories may be debated, the moral essence of the incidences remains consistent. The anecdotes, surrounding Shivba and his illustrating qualities such as wit, courage, resourcefulness, positive approach attributed to him from a very young age, are passed on from generation to generation. The stories or incidences are often cited as examples of Shivba's ability to navigate tricky situations with intelligence and courage. And it was no wonder he could do unimaginable things for the welfare of his people and Swarajya, when he became a king.

It is said that 'Child is a father of the man' truly applies to Shivba, as whatever determination that he showed for freedom and self-rule in his childhood, he achieved it as he grew up. Shivba's stories have become integral parts of the folklore, contributing to the legendary status of this great King. Shivba's early instances of intelligence, courage, and leadership qualities laid the foundation for his future achievements as a great Maratha king and military strategist.

As Shivba grew up and became a teenager, he achieved greater heights of success for Swarajya and became an ever-rising King of people.

6. RAMA AND SHIVBA

Rama is a revered deity in Hindu religion. He is the seventh and one of the most popular incarnations of Lord Vishnu. He was born in Ayodhya, a capital of Kosala kingdom, as son of Kaushalya and King Dashratha. He had three brothers, Lakshman, Bharat and Shatrughna.

Rama took birth as incarnation of Lord Vishnu at the times when Demon king Ravana had wreaked havoc in three lokas or three worlds of the Universe, *Swarg Loka, Mrityu Loka* and *Paatal Loka* or abode of the Asuras (demons). Gods were tormented by the atrocious Ravana so they approached Brahma. Lord Brahma had given a boon to Ravana making him invincible from Deva, Gandharva, Naga, Yaksha, Danavas, who would not be able to kill him. This was except Humans whom Ravana did not include in his prayer to Brahma as he grossly underestimated them. Brahma upon considering the harm caused by Ravana knew that only a human form of life can eliminate Ravana so he turned to Lord Vishnu for the respite. Lord Vishnu was prayed by all the Gods to reincarnate as a human and kill Ravana so the Universe is saved from his wrath.

Ravana was no ordinary demon. Ravana was the son of the sage Vishrava and the Rakshasa princess Kaikesi and paternal grandson of the sage Pulastya, was one of the ten Prajapatis, or mind-born sons of Brahma, and one of the Saptarishi or Seven Great Sages. His maternal grandfather was Sumali or Sumalaya, the king of the Rakshasas and the son of Sukesha. Ravana had seven brothers and two sisters named Kubera, Kumbhkarna, Vibhishana, Khara, Dushana, Ahiravan, Kumbhini, Sahastra Ravana, and Shurpanakha. Kubera, a Yaksha King who ruled Lanka at the behest of Lord Vishnu. Yaksha are class of nature spirits or deities who guard places or treasure, of which some are kind while others may be mischievous. Ravana forced Kubera to flee Lanka after performing penance to Brahma and Shiva and then became the prince of Lanka, and later the ruler, after Sumali's death.

Ravana was a great scholar of Vedas. Ravana was the great devotee of Lord Shiva. Ravana is worshipped as one of Shiva's most revered followers and he is even worshipped in some Shiva temples. Ravana was an excellent ruler and the maestro of the Veena (plucked string instrument). He had written two books, the Ravana Samhita; a book of astrology, and Arka Prakasham; a book of Siddha medicine. Ravana was well-versed in Ayurveda, an ancient medical science and dark practices of black magic. Ravana is said to have the power to control the planetary positions. Ravana owned Pushpakviman, a flying chariot, which he had won from his step-brother Kubera. He was also a master of tantra vidya, the science of creating optical illusions of thoughts, which he used in battles against his enemies.

Once when Ravana's ailing mother Kaikesi could not visit Lord Shiva, he decided to lift Mount Kailash, a heavenly abode of Lord Shiva, and take it to Lanka. This was an arrogance of Ravana which displeased Lord Shiva so he put his toe on the mountain and trapped Ravana beneath. The trapped and humbled Ravana composed the hymn in the praise of Lord Shiva and asked for forgiveness. Lord Shiva was so ecstatic with Ravana's hymn that he started dancing with all fury and passion, a dance called Tandav and the hymn came to be known as Shiva Tandav Stotram, which exists even today.

Ravana attained education in different science, arts and warfare and underwent a colossal Tapasya or penance to please Lord Shiva on the banks of river Narmada. Ravana during his Tapasya was so devoted towards his deity Lord Shiva that he annexed his head and each time he did so, his head grew back and it happened ten times as he continued his penance. Lord Shiva granted ten heads to Ravana which he had sacrificed to please him giving him the name Dashmukha. The ten heads of Dashmukha Ravana symbolizes the six Shastras and the four Vedas that Ravana had mastered which made him a great scholar and one of the most intelligent beings of those times. He was a master of sixty-four types of knowledge and all weaponry arts. Ravana compiled Veda with the relevant musical Svara or notes and his Shiva Tandava Stotra is the most popular hymn ever sung in praise of Lord Shiva.

Ravana is worshipped by some in the Vidisha region of Madhya Pradesh, India, who see him as a savior and a sign of prosperity. They perform daily puja in the Ravana temple and offer *Naivedyam* or *bhog*, a ritual of offering food to the gods. King Shiv Shankar built a Ravana temple in Kanpur, Uttar Pradesh which is opened once a year, on the day of Dussera, to perform puja for the welfare of Ravana. Some communities from Bisrakh, Uttar Pradesh claim their town to be Ravana's birthplace and worship him.

Some sections in Gujarat, India claim to be descendants of Ravana, and some have Ravana as their last names. The Gondi tribe living in Central India claim to be descendants of Ravana, and have temples of Ravana, his wife Mandodari, and their son Meghnad.

On Dussehra, the Gondis from the village of Paraswadi carry an image of Ravana riding on an elephant in a procession in Ravana's honour.

Lord Vishnu did manifest through incarnation of Rama but he wanted to keep only the human form so he could carry out the task entrusted to him by Lord Brahma. Rama's life, as envisioned by Lord Vishnu, was an ideal human life with no divine powers at his disposal, where the spirit of human efforts and emotions of human could take the expression and teach the mankind how they ought to lead their life. Rama was not aware of his divinity till the end of the Battle with Ravana, as Lord Vishnu had envisioned the avatar. Rama did not demonstrate any divine powers and could not change the adversities he faced at the tip of his finger. He was a human being of Mrityu Loka with no magical prowess apart from qualities which Lord Vishnu had envisioned in him. Lord Vishnu desired his incarnation to be a most ideal human being who used his emotions and feelings and suffered in adversities. Lord Rama serves, as the most refined form of human species, for the humans to learn the moral code and devotion towards values to live by. Lord Vishnu wanted to reveal this not merely by stating it but by living it through and through, so it is forever etched for the humans to adhere to it.

Rama was born in a royal family but lead the life of difficult paths and sometimes some insurmountable challenges. He suffered exile of fourteen long years under hard and strenuous circumstances and faced challenges and moral dilemmas.

Rama was married to Sita, the daughter of King Janaka of Mithila. King Janaka had kept the condition that he would marry off his daughter to one who is able to strung Pinaka, the celestial bow gifted to the king by Lord Shiva. The ceremony of *Swayamvar* was arranged where the woman chooses a man for marriage out of the suitors. None of the princes who came for Swayamvar could even lift the bow. When Rama took his turn, he prayed to Lord Shiva to let him lift the celestial bow. Rama did not only lift and strung the bow but broke it in two halves. Thrilled King Janaka, sent for King Dashratha and arranged for the grand wedding of Rama and his dear daughter Sita. Rama and Sita were married in a grand and spectacular wedding ceremony attended by the Kings and Queens from all the kingdoms. It was a joyous moment for the royal family of King Dashratha and the people of Ayodhya.

The things, however, did not remain good for Rama and Sita. King Dashratha had three queens, Kausalya, Sumitra and Kaikeyi. Kausalya was the mother of Rama, Sumitra to twins Lakshman and Shatrughna and Kaikeyi was mother of Bharat.

King Dashratha once in a celestial battle against Sambasura was saved by Kaikeyi who was his charioteer then. She took King Dashratha away from the battlefield and helped him heal from his wounds. Indebted, King Dashratha granted Kaikeyi two boons for asking anything she wanted ever from him. When King Dashratha revealed his decision to coronate Rama as the next king of Ayodhya, Kaikeyi's maid named Manthara, who took care of Kaikeyi since her childhood and was a mother figure for Kaikeyi, convinced Kaikeyi that it was the right time to ask for two boons that King Dashratha had granted to her. Kaikeyi was filled with fear by Manthara that her son Bharat will also remain a servant for Rama if she does not make her son the King of Ayodhya. Misled by Manthara and her blind love for her son Bharat, Kaikeyi asked for two boons - first, Bharat may be coronated as King of Ayodhya and second, Rama may be sent to exile into the forests for fourteen years. King Dashratha, fell in despair over such boons asked by Kaikeyi at such a time. He was morally bound by his words and could never deny Kaikeyi what she was entitled to. King Dashratha unwillingly had to grant the boon and sent Rama into exile for fourteen years.

Sita accompanied her husband Rama wherever he was destined to do. His brother Lakshman also went along with Rama to the forests in exile despite of Rama being reluctant on taking the path alone. Kaikeyi's son Bharat refused to be a king and instead kept Rama's paduka (wooden footwear) on the throne and ruled Ayodhya only as a caretaker till Rama returned from his exile.

Rama, Sita and Lakshman went into the forests and had their challenges surviving during the exile. They fought demons and did good for the people who adored him. Later, they reached Panchavati, very beautiful five gardens, in Dandaka jungle, in present day Nashik, Maharashtra, where they found abode. They built their hermitage and stayed peacefully till one fine day Ravana's sister Shurpanakha came there and saw the handsome Rama and insisted him on marrying her. Rama told her that he was married but she can ask his brother Lakshman. Shurpanakha found offence and tried to assault Sita and that is when Lakshman intervened and cut her nose. The place derived a name Nasika or nose which later came to be known as Nashik. Shurpanakha was the sister of mighty Ravana whom she narrated the incidence. Ravana got furious on hearing the humiliation and cutting of nose of his sister. So, he hatched a plan to abduct Sita with the help of Maricha, a demon and maternal uncle of Ravana, who could create illusions and assume any form he wanted to create trickery. Maricha appeared before Sita as a golden deer. Sita was mesmerized by the beauty of the deer which she had never seen before, so he asked Rama to get hold of the deer so she could pet the deer.

Rama chased the golden deer and caught hold of it only to realize that it has turned into a demon Maricha. The demon called out 'Oh Sita, Oh Lakshman' mimicking Rama's voice to create delusion that Rama was in trouble. On hearing the loud cry, Sita asked Lakshman to go and help Rama which might be in distress. Maricha died by the arrow hit by Rama. Lakshman refused to leave Sita alone but had to comply with Sita's command. Lakshman drew a line or *Lakshman Rekha* around the hermitage to protect Sita and requested her not to cross the *Rekha.* Ravana appeared before Sita disguised as a sage and asked her for alms. Sita would not have refused alms to a sage and Ravana was aware of this. Ravana asked Sita come out of the Rekha so he could take the alms. As soon as Sita came out, Ravana revealed himself and took Sita forcefully in his *Pushpak Viman* before Rama and Lakshman could return to their hermitage.

Ravana encountered *Jatayu* on his way to Lanka after abducting Sita. Jatayu was a demi-god and the nephew of *Garuda* (an eagle deity and mount or vahana of Lord Vishnu). The Aranya-Kanda or the Forest episode of the Ramayana mentions that Jatayu is the 'King of Vultures' who tried to rescue Sita from Ravana. Jatayu tried to appealed to Ravana's sense of duty and dissuade Ravana from such a deplorable act but Ravana did not pay heed to it. The combat ensued where old Jatayu fought valiantly with Ravana. Ravana used Chandrahas sword, once given to him by Lord Shiva, to attack Jatayu and defeated him. Ravana clipped Jatayu's wings due to which Jatayu descended upon the earth. Rama and Lakshaman, while searching for Sita, found the stricken and dying Jatayu. Jatayu told them about his battle with Ravana who had headed south with Sita in his *Pushpak Viman.* Jatayu then died of his wounds and Rama performed his final funeral rites. The distraught Rama, in compassion for the brave Jatayu, uttered the words, 'Le Pakshi!' (Rise, oh bird!).

Later, Rama and Lakshman met an old lady ascetic named Shabari who was bright and knowledgeable saint. She had nothing to offer to Rama so she got berries meticulously plucked for Rama. She would taste the berry to check if it was sweet before she kept it in her basket. Shabari discarded the bitter ones and kept only the sweet ones in her basket. She did not know that the offerings could not be tasted. Rama ate the berries without any hesitation although Lakshman raised a concern. Rama said that anything offered to him with love was a worthy offering. Shabari helped Rama find Sugriva, a king of Vanara (monkey or apes) kingdom of Kishkindha.

Rama and Lakshman met Hanuman, an incarnation of Lord Shiva as per Shiv Puran. He is a greatest devotee of Rama and *Chiranjivi* or immortal who would live on Earth till the end of Kali Yug. Hanuman is a son of Lord Vayu who, as a small child, leaped at the Sun thinking of it as ripe fruit. He was blessed with many boons from the Gods making him the most powerful. Hanuman, Sugriva and his nephew, Angad, led the Vanara sena to find where Sita was kept and then built the bridge Ram Setu or Ram's Bridge to reach Lanka. Ram Setu was built with floating rocks and exists even today.

Hanuman met Ravana in his royal court at Lanka, as a messenger of Rama. Ravana in his fury, ordered his demons to set Hanuman's tail on fire and take him on the streets of Lanka. They wrapped Hanuman's tail with cloth and soaked in oil and set it on fire. Hanuman, the immortal, with the burning tail set ablaze the Lanka to teach a lesson to Ravana. It can be said that Hanuman alone was enough to kill Ravana and bring back Sita but it was Rama who was destined do this task.

Kamban Ramayana narrates that Rama wanted to establish a Shiva Linga in Rameshwaram and was looking for a priest familiar with the traditions. So, Jambavan, the mystical king of bears and a minister of Sugriva, told that it was a challenging task to find a priest there to do the Yajna, a ritual before the sacred fire. However, he said that the only person who could do this Yajna was Ravana, the grandson of Pulastya Rishi. Lord Ram asked Jambavan to approach Ravana and ask him if we would act as a priest in the Yajna.

Jambavan was a friend of Pulastya Rishi, so Ravana asked the Rakshashs to line up in the streets with their hands folded to lead Jambavan towards the palace.

Ravana touched Jambavan's feet and welcomed him to Lanka. Jambavan told Ravana who was the Yajamana for whom the Yajna was to be performed and also that the purpose of the Yajna was to consecrate a Shivlinga and seek blessings for victory over Lanka. Ravana agreed to perform the Yajna and also get all the essential items for the Yajna as Rama was doing the Yajna in a forest.

Rama, as instructed by Ravana, took a bath and was ready at daybreak. Ravana came to the other side of the ocean from Lanka in his Pushpak Viman the next day. He had told Sita that she would have to attend the Yajna as Rama's wife must sit with him to complete the Yajna.

Rama greeted him and told him why he was doing his Yajna. Hanuman had gone to Kailasha to bring a Shivalinga, Ravana explained that they could no longer delay the Yajna and asked Rama to be seated. Ravana then asked Rama to send Vibheeshan to the Pushpak Vimana and accompany Sita so that she could participate in the Yajna. Rama and Sita completed the Yajna and consecrated the Shivlinga, which is known as the Lankeshwar Shivlinga, present today in Rameshwaram. When Hanuman returned from Kailash, the Shivlinga he brought was placed adjacent to this linga.

Ram and Sita bowed to Ravana, who blessed Sita by

saying '*Akhanda Soubhagyawati Bhava*,' which translated to 'may you always be the one whose husband is alive.' Rama and Sita asked him for his Dakshina. Ravana said 'What can they offer the king of the golden city of Lanka?' but when Rama insisted, Ravana asked Rama to be present before his eyes at the time of his death.

Rama took his Vanara sena to Lanka. Ravana's son Meghnad or Indrajit, a mighty and powerful warrior, his brother *Kumbhkaran,* and many great demons fought and perished in the battle. Meghnad used *Nagasatra* (snake weapon) on Rama so Lord Vishnu's mount Garuda came to the battlefield and ate the weapons. Lakshman was however hit by Shakti arrow of Meghnad and fell unconscious. Hanuman was sent to bring Sanjivani herb from Himalayas so he went and picked up the *Dronagiri* Mountain and brought it to Lanka and it saved Lakshman and other injured Vanaras.

A huge battle was fought between the Vanara sena of Rama and the demons of Ravana which ended with the end of Ravana. When Ravana was dying, Rama sent Lakshmana to listen to him. Ravana gave teachings that were codified in a text called Ravana Gita.

Rama brought Sita back to Ayodhya. Sita had to undergo second exile while she was pregnant so she takes refuge at hermitage of Sage Valimiki and delivers two sons Luv and Kush. The sons reunite with their father after they grow up with their mother Sita. Later, Sita sought final refuge in the arms of mother Bhumi or Earth, which splits open and takes Sita along.

Ram Rajya or rule of Lord Ram, over his kingdom is known as pious kingdom for the people and considered the most ideal and morally highest rule in the Universe. Ram Rajya is synonymous to the rule where there is prosperity, peace and happiness among people and the King is virtuous and faithful to the interest of the people who would sacrifice his life to keep his people safe.

Similarly, Shivba was destined to set up a Ram Rajya or Swarajya, for the righteous rule for the people who were in darkness and needed a saviour to bring them out of their miseries. Both Lord Rama and Shivba are revered figures in Indian history and culture. While they belong to different eras, there are certain similarities in their lives and the qualities they possessed that resonate with people.

It is notable that Rama and Shivba both were naughty as children and played pranks on others. Rama would chase a calf in the palace courtyard and play the entire day. The king Dashratha, on setting down for his meals, would call Rama but Rama would not come for food. His mother Kaushalya would run behind Rama but she could hardly catch hold of him. Rama would come on his own with hands besmeared in dust and slush, took a bite or two and again run away.

Shivba too would not come for meals and play instead until he was caught hold of by Jijabai or the nannies. Shivba loved to play pranks and hide so they could not find him. Kaushalya and Jijabai, both could not completely attend their household chores because of their naughty sons.

Both Rama and Shivba were deeply devoted to their respective ideals. The sense of commitment to Dharma or righteousness was deeply rooted in them. Rama was known as Maryada Purshottam or the perfect man for the qualities he displayed as a righteous king, obedient son, loving husband and respectful even as an enemy. Shivba had deeply ingrained devotion towards Dharma which he had absorbed from the values from Garbha Sanskar which means teachings given to the child during the pregnancy of the mother. Jijabai would call and refer to Shivba as Raje or a king, when he was in her womb. His learnings came from a courageous, astute and a brilliant mother which helped him become a victorious king when he grew up.

Both Rama and Shivba had unshakeable faith in their deities. Although Rama was a divine soul, he was humble enough to bow before a saint or ascetic and abided by their wishes. Rama had such profound influence on Shivba that he had named his second son as Ram who later came to be known as Rajaram, who was a great king. Shivba was a devout Hindu and had a strong faith in his family deity, the Goddess Bhavani. His devotion to his mission of establishing Swarajya was blessed to triumph by Goddess Bhavani.

Rama was an innately brave and so was Shivba. Rama's extraordinary strength and courage, even as a child, is evident from how he once saved the sage Vishwamitra's sacrificial rites from the demons Mareecha and Subahu. Similarly, Shivba fought his first battle when he was just fifteen years old and won over his enemies displaying valour and grit. Rama was the protector of his subjects and fought against anything that could harm his people. Shivba had resolved to protect his people and the Holy cows, Vedas, and Brahmans (holy men, scholars and priests, not any caste) and so he was also called *Gou Brahman Pratipaalak*, which means the protector of the above three.

Lord Rama, the ideal king or *Rajadhiraja*, was known for his just and fair rule in the kingdom of Ayodhya. Similarly, Shivba was a staunch follower of the principles of equality and justice. Shivba later came to be regarded as an exemplary king in history of India, known for his innovative and extraordinary military strategies, administrative policies and reforms, and his pure vision of a prosperous, equitable kingdom.

Both Rama and Shivba were valiant warriors who

displayed immense courage and prowess in the battles they fought during their lifetime. Rama slayed powerful demons and killed Ravana showing the bravery and strength that no one else had. Shivba slayed the armed, dangerous and cunning Adil Shah sardar called Afzal Khan, in one-to-one combat, when the odds were completely against him showcasing extraordinary military brilliance and fearlessness.

Both Rama and Shivba displayed immense respect for women. Lord Rama's devotion to Sita and his unwavering commitment to her is known to all. Shivba was very devoted to his wife Saibai, mother of his great warrior son, Sambhaji or as he was fondly called Shambhu Raje. Shivba had lost Saibai to illness when Sambhaji was only two years old, after which Sambhaji was raised by Jijabai. Both Rama and Shivba lost their consort earlier in their lifetime. Rama highly regarded women and it is evident from many incidences of his lifetime such as Shabari and forgiveness to Kaikeyi and Manthara. Shivba, too, held women in high regard and respected their dignity and there are countless accounts where he has shown great respect for women. He established stringent laws to protect women and their honor in Swarajya.

Rama and Shivba came from royal and blessed families and could have lived their lives in richness but both these heroes stepped out of their comforts for their own people and undertook a massive challenge to correct the circumstances by their own persistent and devoted efforts.

Both of them were skilled warriors and were excellent Archers. Shivba, at one instance when he became a king, appeared in the battle of Umberkhind, against the Mughal general Kartalab Khan, dressed in his perfect milk-white Angarakha with his bow slung on the right shoulder, riding on a mighty horse and two quivers full of arrows, one on each side of the horse, resembling the virtuous and invincible Lord Rama himself.

While the historical contexts of Lord Rama and Shivba are different, the values they embody, such as courage, righteousness, and devotion, make them revered figures in Indian cultural and religious traditions. Both Rama and Shivba have left a lasting impact on the collective consciousness of the Indian people, symbolizing ideals of leadership, valour, and virtues.

7. KRISHNA AND SHIVBA

Krishna is another revered deity in Hindu religion just like Rama. He is the eighth avatar and again one of the most popular incarnations of Lord Vishnu. He is a centrical figure in Mahabharata, Bhagavata Purana, Brahma Vaivarta Purana, Bhagavad Gita, and is mentioned in various Hindu philosophical and mythological texts.

Lord Vishnu incarnated himself as Lord Krishna in the Dwapara Yuga for two important happenings, first, Lord Krishna defeated his evil maternal uncle, Kansa, and secondly, he was the guide of the Pandavas during the battle of Kurukshetra. Krishna was a purna avatar, which means a complete incarnation as he had sixteen kalas or divine qualities. So, for this reason, he was called '*16 kala sampurna*'. Rama, on the other hand, was a purna avatar but was *'14 kala sampurna'* as he had to hid two kalas or divine qualities in order to be a human being to be able to kill Ravana as per Lord Brahma's boon to Ravana. The two kalas hidden by Rama were being Paripurna (complete knowledge of all forms of awakening) and Swarupavasthit (established in his real true self).

Lord Vishnu had envisioned the avatar of Krishna in a different light of his divinity. Krishna was completely aware that he was incarnation of Lord Vishnu and what was his purpose of birth.

Krishna literally means black or dark as a cloud. Krishna is born to mother Devaki and father Vasudeva, who belonged to the Yadava clan in Mathura. Krishna had two siblings, named Balarama and Subhadra. Devaki's cousin named Kansa was the tyrant king of the Vrishni kingdom, with its capital at Mathura. The Puranas describe him as an asura or as an asura reborn in the body of a man.

Kamsa was a son of King Ugrasena and Queen Padmavati. He was over-ambitious and had personal confidantes or advisers named Banasura and Narakasura. Kamsa, acting upon the advisers decided to overthrow his father, and coronate himself as the King of Mathura. Later, upon following another advisor, Chanura, Kamsa decided to marry Asti and Prapti, the daughters of Jarasandha, King of Magadha. He overthrew his father and became the king of Vrishni kingdom.

Devaki was married to Yadava prince Vasudeva, son of Yadava king Shurasena. After the marriage ceremony, Kansa volunteered to escort the newly wedded Devaki and Vasudev to Mathura and drove their chariot himself. At that time, a celestial voice or Akashvani (voice from the skies) prophesied that Devaki's eighth son would kill Kansa and free the land from his rule. Kansa was infuriated by thos prophecy and rose to kill Devaki. Vasudev stopped Kansa and promised him that he would give each child to him whom he would kill.

Kansa imprisoned Devaki and Vasudeva, and killed all of their children at their birth. However, just before the birth of the seventh child of Devaki and Vasudeva, Vishnu told the goddess Mahamaya to transfer the child from the womb of Devaki to that of Rohini, another wife of Vasudeva. Rohini gave birth to Devaki's seventh son, named Balarama.

The eighth son, Krishna, an avatar of Vishnu, was born in the prison of Kansa, at midnight on a dark and stormy night in the month of Shravana. Vasudeva and Devaki were terrified of the fate of the newborn child as Kansa had huge number of guards and kept an eye particularly on the birth of Devaki's eighth child. Vasudeva and Devaki heard the prophecy that the eighth child had taken birth and to take him to Gokul by crossing the Yamuna River to Nanda, who was the head of cowherd, and replace the newborn son with the newborn daughter of Nanda and bring her along with him.

Vasudeva's shackles broke and prison gates open as the guards fell asleep. Vasudeva took the child in his arms and set out in the stormy and dark night. River Yamuna was flooded; the bridge was washed away and no boats could cross the river. The despaired Vasudeva entered the flooding river holding the newborn baby above his head. Shesh Nag, a huge serpent appeared and spread its five hoods to protect his Lord Vishnu' incarnation. As soon as water touched the baby's feet, it subsided and allowed Vasudeva to cross the river. Amidst all the chaos, the baby was calm and sucked the toe of his left foot.

Vasudeva, went on to find Nanda's house who was the chief of cowherds in Gokul. There was a silence in Gokul. It was pouring and no one was awake. Vasudeva found Nanda's house where Nanda and Yashoda were in deep sleep. He placed Krishna next to Yashoda and took her newborn daughter and left for Mathura. It was the grace of Krishna that the daughter was replaced with this mystic child. Nanda and Yashoda were unknowingly made foster parents of Krishna.

Vasudeva returned to his captivity in Kansa's Mathura. The guards woke up and informed Kansa about the birth of the eighth child. Kansa was anxious and wanted to kill this child as soon as he could. Devaki pleaded to Kansa that it was a daughter and so he should let her go. But Kansa would not take any chance, whether it was a son or daughter, he wanted to kill the child. When Kansa tried to kill the child, it slipped his hands and flew up in the air and told Kansa that he could not kill her as she was Goddess Yogamaya and the one who would kill him has taken birth on earth.

Kansa was adamant on finding the eighth child and killing him so he sent a host of asuras like Aghasura, Bakasura, Kaliye and Putana to Gokul to kill Krishna, but Krishna killed each one of them. Finally, Krishna arrived in Mathura when Kansa invited him and Balarama and many others for wrestling match. Kansa told Kootaka to get his ferocious and violent elephant named as Kuvalayapida to kill Krishna as soon as he enters the gates of the wrestling arena. Kuvalayapida charged at Krishna when he entered the wrestling ring but Krishna sliced his trunk.

Kansa sent his huge and unbeatable wrestler Chanura to kill Krishna during the wrestling match, which was against the rules of Bahuyuddha or traditional wrestling. Krishna however defeated Chanura and Balaram defeated Mushtika, another great wrestler of Kansa.

Kansa, got his contingent of Jarasandha's Magadha soldiers in his palace and attacked Krishna. There was a chaos and stampede as people, who were baffled by this sudden attack, started running haphazardly. Kansa stepped in to kill Krishna and that is when Krishna saw Kansa holding a sword in fury and running towards him. Akrura, Krishna's uncle, tried to stop Kansa but he was knocked away by Kansa. Kansa came close to Krishna. Krishna ran up to Kansa and held him by his hair and pulled him down. Kansa fell down and dropped his sword. Krishna dragged Kansa into the wrestling ring and then he took Kansa's sword. Kansa was trying to get hold of Krishna. Then Krishna, for the sake of people and Mathura which was suffering under the tyrant Kansa, beheaded Kansa with his own sword. Krishna was only eleven and a half years old when he slayed Kansa.

Krishna is the one of the most adored deities in Hinduism. He is depicted wearing a peacock-feather crown or a single feather on his head, and playing Bansuri or the Indian flute. He is seen with cows or a calf, or he is seen as a romantic young boy with the *gopis* or milkmaids. Krishna is also seen on the battlefield of the epic Mahabharata. He chose to be a charioteer to the Pandava prince Arjuna and told Bhagavad Gita, a scripture of Hinduism.

Krishna is known for his Leela or the divine play as a baby when he was growing up in Gokul. Balkrishna or Krishna as a child is seen as a toddler crawling on his hands and knees, sometimes a dancing child, and at other times an innocent-looking child playfully stealing or consuming butter for which he is called as *Makkhan*

Chor. Krishna as an infant is always shown holding Laddu in his hand.

Krishna is called *Vatapatrasayi* or Lord of the Banyan Leaf. Once a great sage Markendaya, was sitting on the bank of the river Subhadra for his evening worship, at the point where the river met the sea. The sea began to swell and rise leading into a cosmic flood which swept the sage away, but he did not drown him. It was Pralaya or the waters of cosmic dissolution in which the whole Universe began to submerge. It drowned the continents and every mountain, forest, river and valley. The Universe was drowning into the ocean as Markandeya was floating along. He saw that there was nothing left and there was a huge ocean on all sides ready to swallow the Universe and end the humanity. Just then he saw a leaf of the Banyan tree floating in the water. There was a small baby on the banyan leaf, which was Krishna, sucking the lotus-like toe of his right foot, unlike the left toe when he had crossed Yamuna as a newborn. The water subsided; everything went to normal as the universe had restored to the source.

Krishna is seen in his different forms in different regions, such as Jagannatha in Odisha, Vithoba in Maharashtra, Shrinathji in Rajasthan and Guruvayoorappan in Kerala.

Krishna and Shivba were very similar to each other,

particularly in their childhoods. Krishna and Shivba had been born in adverse political conditions. They both had enemies on a prowl to kill them before their births. Even after their birth, enemies did not cease their pursuit and they faced the peril of being found and eliminated. Yashoda and Jijabai protected their children from the possible threats of the foes and displayed exceptional bravery. For Krishna, being Lord Vishnu himself, he may not have been harmed, but Yashoda had to face the gruesome and horrific attacks on her son. Jijabai, too, knew what would be the consequences if Sultanate forces would lay hands on Shivba.

Both, Krishna and Shivba were very naughty as children. It exactly was the case with Rama too. They had friends with whom they used to play fun pranks with each other and also with others. Krishna was fond of eating butter which Yashoda would tie high above the ground so Krishna does not over-eat it. Krishna would call his friends to climb one on top of the other to form a pyramid just to reach the pot of butter. Krishna would get down the butter pot and relished it with all his friends.

Krishna as a toddler would play in the garden with his elder brother Balaram. Just like Shivba did as a baby, Krishna used to pick up soft mud and stuff it in his mouth. Once the children saw Krishna putting mud in his mouth and they complained to his mother.

Mother Yashoda came to Krishna and asked him whether he had eaten mud or not. Krishna shook his head and say no. Yashoda asked him to open his mouth, which Krishna reluctantly did. Yashoda looked inside his mouth and saw the whole universe inside the Lord himself.

Krishna and Shivba both shared a great love for horses. They had horses and kept them in the stables with care and compassion. Shivba knew that the horses were the foundation of his army and always instructed his commanders to keep horses in good health and condition. Krishna, on the battlefield of Kurukshetra, was the charioteer for Arjuna and the chariot was drawn by four white horses named Saibya, Sugriva, Meghapushpa, and Balahaka. Krishna ensured that the horses were well-fed and rested and would personally brush the dirt off horses' coats, groom the horses, pick out the hooves, and feed them with the top-grade grains and grass. During the battle, Krishna cautioned Arjuna that the horses were tired and wounded and needed water. There was no water around so Arjuna shot an arrow on the ground and water gushed out so the horses could drink it.

Krishna had friends from all sections of the community. He, just like Shivba, did not see if their friend was rich or poor, powerful or weak. Krishna's friend Sudama, who was a poor Brahmin, went to meet Krishna at Dwarka and when he returned, he saw that his hut was transformed into a golden palace with beautiful park and gardens. Similarly, Shivba had many childhood friends who, one like Tanaji Malusare as a poor child came to the Shivba's Lal Mahal at Pune remained forever with Shivba.

Krishna advised Arjuna to fight the battle to protect the Dharma, or righteousness, against those who stood with Adharma, or unrighteousness, and also told him that if he died fighting this battle, his soul will remain immortal. In the same way, Maharaja Chhatrasal, King of Bundelkhand came really inspired to Shivba, a Chhatrapati then, for his guidance. Shivba told him that as he raises his banner of revolt against Mughals, he is fighting the battle to protect the Dharma and if he died fighting this battle, his soul will remain immortal. Maharaja Chhatrasal learned some military techniques from Shivba, one of which was Archery. At the time of departure, Shivba told Maharaja Chhatrasal that he is victorious because he is blessed by Goddess Bhavani but if he wants to win this war against the enemies, he should remember Lord Krishna.

Both Krishna and Shivba were known for their strategic acumen. Krishna played a key role in devising strategies during the Kurukshetra War, as described in the Bhagavad Gita. Krishna knew the strengths and weaknesses of each and every warrior that ever stepped on the battleground of Kurukshetra. Dronacharya, was a powerful and valiant warrior in Kurukshetra who, also a Guru or teacher of Pandavas and Kauravas, sided with Kauravas in the war being duty-bound towards the throne of Hastinapur. Dronacharya started using deadly celestial weapons like Brahmastra against the common and ordinary soldiers of Pandavas which was against the rules of war.

Krishna had to get rid of Dronacharya but he had vowed not to pick weapon in the battle and became a charioteer of Arjuna. Bhima killed the elephant named Ashwatthama and claimed that he has killed Dronacharya's son with the same name. Dronacharya went to confirm the claim with Yudhishthira, who was known for his adherance to Dharma and honesty. Yudhisthira, who was instructed by Krishna, said 'Narova Kunjarova' meaning 'Ashwatthama is dead, but whether a human or the elephant, I don't know'. This broke Dronacharya and he descended his chariot and laid down his weapons. Before the Pandavas could arrest him, the enraged Dhrishtadyumna unexpectedly beheaded Dronacharya as a revenge for killing his father Drupada, a king of Panchala kingdom.

Shivba, too, was a brilliant military strategist and knew the strengths and weaknesses of his enemies in unbelievably small details. When Shivba became a king and his kingdom began to rise, Adil Shah sent his cruel and tyrant commander named Afzal Khan to capture Shivba, 'dead or alive' but Afzal Khan had all the plans to kill Shivba at the first instance. Not surprisingly, Shivba had read his intentions right and knew that

Afzal Khan's invasion was the biggest threat to Swarajya as he had set out to wipe out the relatively smaller kingdom of Swarajya. Afzal Khan had taken a vow in the court of Adil Shah that he will bring Shivba to the same court and prove himself. The warrior who was ready to take up a royal challenge was supposed to pick a rolled-up betel leaf from a plate presented to him. It was called as *Paijecha Vida* or a token of challenge, symbolic or actual, taken up by a warrior.

Shivba knew that Afzal Khan was a cunning commander who had been a Subhedar of Wai for twelve years and knew the region well. He had killed his sixty wives before he started for the expedition against Shivba so that if they do not marry anyone else in his absence. He had got Shivba's elder brother killed and had also imprisoned Shahaji Raje by conspiracy. Afzal Khan desecrated the holy temple of Tuljapur and destroyed all the temples on his way.

Shivba told his diplomat Gopinath Pant Bokil to meet Afzal Khan and persuade him to come to Pratapgad along with only ten bodyguards. Just like Krishna told Yudhisthira, Shivba told Gopinath Pant to tell Afzal Khan that Shivba was scared and wanted to meet and draw a truce with him to get him where he could be killed. Afzal Khan indeed came to Pratapgad with only ten bodyguards and was killed in one-on-one combat at the hands of Shivba.

Shivba was an ace Archer just like Krishna. Krishna once went for a Swayamvar where Princess Lakshmana's father announced that the warrior who could hit the eye of the fish will marry Lakshmana. Jarasandha, Duryodhana and an archer as great as Arjuna missed the target. Krishna was able to hit the target and could marry Lakshmana and make her his consort. Shivba and Krishna were both great Archers who manifested their skill in the battle against Adharma.

Krishna and Shivba displayed compassion and utmost concern for their people. Krishna was often described as a reservoir of compassion and a leader guiding his devotees towards Dharma. Krishna saved Draupadi's dignity by miraculously elongating her saree when Dushasana tried to disrobe her by dragging her in the court after a fateful game of dice was won by Kauravas. Krishna helped his poor friend Sudama and also protected people of Vrindavan from wrath of Lord Indra in the form of rainstorm, by lifting Govardhan mountain on his little finger. Krishna met Trivarka or Kubja, his devotee in Mathura who offered him sandalwood paste, from her hunchback. Kubja turned into a beautiful woman and had been cursed in her previous birth which Krishna liberated her from.

Krishna's cousin and son of his aunt Shrutasubh was named Shishupal. It was foretold that he would be killed by Krishna. So, Krishna made a promise to

Shrutasubha that he will pardon a hundred sins of Shishupal. It was only when Shishupal committed a hundred sins and insulted Krishna time and again, Krishna released Sudarshan Chakra on Shishupal and liberated his soul to attain salvation.

Similarly, Shivba was known for his just and empathetic rule for his people. He made policies that ensured the welfare of his people and strived to relieve the suffering of the common masses. Shivba gave a humane treatment to prisoners of war and never killed any enemy soldier once he has surrendered himself and laid down his weapons. He rendered for the well-being of captured enemy soldiers and, in sometimes even let them enlist themselves in his own service.

Shivba showed a lot of religious tolerance and ensured the protection to people of all faiths and brought harmony to the people. He was compassionate towards poor and gave away a lot of his wealth in charity and helping the downtrodden people. The untouchability was very high in those times but Shivba was the first person to break the norms of untouchability and employ Dalit soldiers in his army. He removed the caste discrimination and gave everyone equal opportunity. The soldiers were called *Mavala* irrespective of their social status, caste, class or religion. Shivba was compassionate about all the religions including Islam and never made enemies or waged war solely for the reason of religion.

The great poet Bhushan or known Kavi Bhushan, has made many poems about Shivba where he calls him a *Kalpavriksha*, a divine wish-fulfilling tree. He says that when you come to Shivba, he grants more than what you wished for. Many other poets and writers have stated that it is more fulfilling to be a peasant in Shivba's Swarajya than being a king of any other kingdom. Shivba's compassion and the acts of generosity and charity were known across Bharatvarsh at the time.

There was another similarity between Krishna and Shivba. And that was the sense of enterprising. They had a terrific sense of allotting and utilizing whatever resources they had to turn them into an opportunity for welfare for people. Krishna was the foster son of the head of cowherds and lived in Vrindavan, an ancient pastoral village. Vrindavan was known for its immense wealth and a highly advanced culture where cows formed its backbone. The butter, yoghurt, curd, milk, ghee, etc. was produced at Vrindavan making it rich and prosperous. The responsibilities of running the enterprise were divided among several members of the community; the young boys or men herded the cows and calves and took them for grazing; young women helped with milking the cows and churning the butter; elder women prepared the products to be sold and; elder men took them to the market and sold the goods. Vrindavan always kept flourishing and prospering under the rule of Krishna.

Shivba, just like Krishna, had impeccable sense of using his resources, which were limited when he started, to utilize them into the service for kingdom. He did not have much to start Swarajya but during his lifetime, he had transformed it into one of the richest kingdoms in India.

Aurangzeb and many other kings, on the other hand, went broke at the time of their deaths. Aurangzeb, who ruled for forty-nine years and died at the age of eighty-eight, died a miserable death and only had Rupees Three Hundred at his disposal when he died. The descendants of Mughals at present live in slums of Kolkata, India.

Shivba taught his people to be self-reliant and believe in their own hard work and efforts. His descendants lived the life of morals and Swarajya's wealth lasted for centuries to come. Shivba never kept anything as a personal wealth or assets. He had dedicated his life for the welfare of people and enriched their lives with his commitment towards Swarajya. Shivba's Swarajya never saw any indiscriminate splurging of wealth on personal pleasures or luxuries. He created a kingdom of moral wealth which thrived and boomed for the generations to come and became a symbol of prosperity and righteousness.

8. SHIVBA AND HIS RESPECT FOR WOMEN

Shivba, the son of a great lady, inherited immensely from his mother. It is primarily from her and his ideal and dignified father that he learned how women should be respected. Shivba grew up with the values that very few had in those times.

During the influence of Mughal rule, women were treated either like a trophy or a burden depending upon which class or social segment they belonged to. They were considered inferior to men in many aspects. Mughals were known for their atrocities and ill-treatment of people under their rule. They were foreign invaders from Mongolia whose sole motive was exploiting the people and accumulate wealth for themselves. They had no purpose of welfare for the people under their rule. They invaded India with intent to extract its enormous wealth and enrich themselves and they did that under the guise of a Mughal kingdom which they had spread among various parts of India.

Hindus, under the Sultanate rule, were oppressed and had no religious or social freedom. They faced atrocities at the whims of the barbarian Islamic rulers who were inhumane towards the people. People were forcefully converted to Islam under the threat of death. The Sultanates went to an extent of imposing the draconian *Jiziya* tax where non-Muslims paid a different tax as a fee for protection provided by the Muslim ruler to non-Muslims and for the permission to practice a non-Muslim faith and as a material proof of the non-Muslims' allegiance to the Muslim state and its laws. In short, there was a tax to be of a faith other than Islam was heavily imposed so people are pushed to convert to Islam. Forceful conversions were rampant and people were harassed to the extent that they had to convert for the sake of their lives.

The situation was grim for even those who possessed wealth and land and had armed men at their disposal. Poor people were helpless and had no respite from the economic, social and religious harassment. The plight of women in these distressing times can only be imagined. Women suffered the most as they became victims of lust by the men of Sultanate rulers. They were tormented at the hands of even the petty soldiers of the Sultanate. The daughters and sisters of Hindus were kidnapped in the broad daylight never to return home. Countless young damsels were abducted from their homes in the presence of their families and pushed into the Harem of Sultans. Harem was a group of women belonging to Sultan who were literally enslaved by abducting, or gifted, presented to or sometimes bought by the Sultans. Ill-fated women ended up in such Harem and could never return to their families. But even the low-ranking officers would forcefully take away women to make them their concubine or slaves. The girls and women were often traded and sold as slaves and sent to Arabic countries. Mostly who tried to escape were found dead or left to die in miserable conditions by the men who abducted them. They were in a state of pity and had no one who would rescue them from the lurking demons.

Common people were traumatized by such brutal and ghastly acts committed under the foreign invaders. They were afraid that they will be met with the same fate with no one to save them. No one wanted to face the wrath of the armed invaders as there were no united front to revolt against the invaders. The commanders of Sultanates were on rampage and showed no mercy to the people as they plundered, looted and scavenged their belongings and forcibly took away their women.

Women were definitely in a state of fear and insecurity as they had no one to shield their dignity and honour. They had the least social security as their well-being was threatened by perils of being taken away and sold and bought almost like a commodity. The Maratha sardars could protect their women as they were in the service of Sultanates and had raised their own small but capable armies for such a service. But nothing guaranteed the safety of their women. A reputed Sardar like Lakhoji Jadhav and his sons were butchered in the broad daylight in the court of Nizamshah so it was difficult to say what could be the fate of the women in their families.

Maratha Sardars were aware of the brutality and lecherousness of the Sultans but only their tight fist on the sword scabbard kept their families unharmed. The demise of any Hindu Sardar or a male patriarch was a spell of curse for the women in the family as it meant fear and a threat of being abducted. No crimes against women were considered so serious by the Mughal Sultanates that it could be exonerated by the influence of their rank or money. Mostly victims' families were bought out by force or wiped out or the victim would finish life with her own hands.

The morality towards women within the Sultanates was at a low and it did not attribute any social stigma to the offender. Sultans themselves had very low morality and blemished conduct towards women that it was considered a norm for a powerful male to have a similar conduct. Infact, the harem of person's wives and concubines became a symbol of his wealth and power. Bigger the harem was, higher the social status of the man. Harem was a secluded area for the women and children in the family but mostly the Sultans turned them into a dungeon where they kept their women slaves and concubines. Women could never get out of this living hell no matter how they ended up there, by constraint or by abduction. The misconduct or even an offence against women was easily condoned if committed by a moderately influential person.

Women, particularly Hindu women, were in pitiful state and lived with no hope of respite from being the prey. And especially those, who were younger and beautiful, were targeted easily and taken away from their families. The absence of a saviour was gravely felt by women for their owns as well as their children. No man or even a kingdom was able to stop these demons from wreaking havoc on innocent women. The question was if the brutal exploitation of women was ever going to stop. No one had an answer to this.

Shivba was born to Jijabai who kept her close to her during his infancy. Shivba witnessed the pain of atrocities on people, particularly on women, through his mother right from when he was in her womb. Jijabai was the wife of a chief general Shahaji Raje who had people serving him and an army at his disposal. People came to Jijabai with their troubles and that is when she bonded with them and understood what they were going through. She would herself see how women were attacked and violated by the Sultanate officers and soldiers. She knew the pain and agony of the women who became victims of such exploitation. Jijabai had a deep resentment towards the ill-treatment accorded to women which turned into anguish over a period of time.

Jijabai, during her pregnancy, witnessed disturbed times and a lot of incidences of violence inciting fear in women about their safety and survival. Men were killed, women were taken away and there was a sense of peril among people. Jijabai saw how women who once worked for her or those she knew for a long time are no longer alive or with their families anymore. Her grief out of seeing women lead miserable and unfortunate lives was intense and the same anguish and resentment was perceived by Shivba in the womb. It was in his existential being that he too despised the ill-treatment towards women and resolved to never tolerate the oppression and abuse of women.

Shivba's court was the only court in Bharatvarsha in those times where no woman has ever danced. It was very common that women dancers entertained the King and his court men. But not where a highly moral king like Shivba ruled. No woman was ever humiliated or disrespected in the Shivba's court. This was in the times when Mughals and other Sultanates were neck-deep in material pleasures, intoxication, gambling and other vices. There was no Sultanate court where the King did not indulge in immoral activities.

Shivba had a strict code of ethics and conduct for every single person in Swarajya. One of the codes was that the women, children, non-combatants and surrendered soldiers shall not be harmed under any circumstances. Shivba put his thoughts into practice and made it known to each and every soldier, officers, commander, ministers and person in Swarajya that women were to be treated with utmost respect and dignity. The violators were harshly punished to deter any such conduct towards women.

Shivba, when he grew up, became a king who did not tolerate immoral conduct towards women and such was his fear among the people that no one dared to harass women under his watch as a king. Shivba did not hesitate to give severe punishment to people who had committed offences against women. He became known till far-off kingdoms for his morality and good conduct towards women and the people in general.

Babaji Bin Bhikaji Gujar

Babaji Bin Bhikaji Gujar was the Mokdum or Patil ('village headman') of the village called as Ranjhe. Babaji was an authoritative person of the village and he did a misconduct with a woman in Ranjhe village. Shivba came to know about it so he sent his men to arrest and bring Babaji before himself. Babaji was given a fair chance and only when his misconduct was proven, Shivba gave him the punishment. Shivba was quick in giving rewards for a good deed and also a punishment for any bad deed which earned him respect in his people. He would never delay justice to anyone under any circumstances otherwise that would serve no purpose to the one who pleaded for justice. Shivba believed in fairness, equality and upholding the rule of law, while also having compassion and empathy at the same time. His sense of justice was excellent and he understood how it served well in any situation.

Babaji's *Mokdumi* or headmanship was confiscated at the moment he was found guilty which stripped him off of his authority. Both of Babaji's hands and legs were cut off which made him a *chaurang* (a short wooden square-stool) as they used to call it in those days. But Babaji was alive after this punishment as it was not a death penalty. Babaji had no children so he was left at his relative named Sonji Bin Banaji Gujar who stayed near Purandar fort.

Sonji came to Shivba and told that he has to take care of Babaji and he has no adequate means to do that and asked to be granted to him the headmanship of Ranjhe village which was earlier granted to Babaji. Shivba generously granted the headmanship to Sonji so he could take care of Babaji.

The episode of Babaji Bin Bhikaji Gujar was an important incidence for serving as a deterrent for decades and brought down the violations against women significantly as people remembered this before laying their finger on any woman. Babaji was etched in the minds of people that Shivba was intolerant of immoral conduct and will impose a punishment that every person dreaded. Babaji Bin Bhikaji Gujar lived on to become a living example of Shivba's fair justice to safeguard the dignity of women. Shivba was only sixteen years old when this incidence had taken place.

Rangoba Trimbak Vadke

The incidence of Babaji Gujar set an example that deterred the offenders from committing crimes against women as everyone knew that Shivba showed no tolerance towards it. There were a very few crimes against women after the punishment given to Babaji Gujar, as found from the old letters during the reign of Shivba.

Yet, there was a village chieftain of Tape village in sub-region called as Mose Khore in Maval region near Pune. The name of this village headman was Rangoba Trimbak Vadke also known as Rangotrimal who committed a similar offence against a woman. His misconduct against a woman came to be known to villagers who further informed Shivba about it. Shivba ordered his men to arrest Rangoba Vadke and bring him before him to know the truth. But Rangoba knew that his offence will be proven and he will be severely punished just like Babaji Gujar. Rangoba who was guilty of the offence ran away and sought refuge at Javali located near Mahabaleshwar near Pune, the region where Chandrarao More was ruling. Shivba had helped Chandrarao More in establishing his kingdom at Javali but he had betrayed Shivba and started committing acts against Swarajya.

Rangoba thought it was safe to be in Javali as Chandrarao More had turned against Shivba and he will protect him. He was right about Chandrarao More as he indeed got refuge at Javali. But Rangoba was not at peace as he knew that Shivba would never forgive his misdeed. Rangoba was anxious and so fearful that every time he heard a sound of footsteps, he would think that Shivba's soldiers have arrived to catch him. The probability of being caught and punished led Rangoba to be so terrified and horrified that he died out of his fear.

This incidence shows us how Shivba's sense of dignity of women and justice towards them was known to each and every person of his kingdom. There was a fear of committing crimes against women as they knew Shivba will not forgive it. Shivba kept his morals and ideals so high that there was nothing that could break or bend his resolve.

Kalyan Raid

In October 1667, Shivba's army raided Kalyan, near Mumbai, which had been captured by Bijapur Sultanate after the fall of Ahmednagar Sultanate. Shivba was in Pune at that time and he had sent a cavalry led by commander called as Abaji Sondev. Shivba had a strong hold on Pune by then so he wanted to expand in Konkan area by seizing the areas held by Bijapur and Mughal Sultanates.

The army sent on the mission by Shivba captured the Kalyan, Thane and Bhiwandi forts under the leadership of Abaji Sondev and got hold of the treasures which they could seize in the raids. They also arrested a few people, among which was the Bijapur Governor Mulla Ahmed's young daughter-in-law, who was extremely beautiful. Abaji Sondev saw the lady and thought it would be worthy to present her before Shivba. It was normal or rather expected in those times that whatever was captured during the army raid was presented to the King, be it jewels, gold, and horses or other valuables. Men were arrested and sent to prison or sent to laborious tasks while Women were made slaves. But this was a great mistake of Abaji Sondev.

As soon as Mulla Ahmed's young daughter-in-law was presented before Shivba, everyone in the court was surprised as this was not a common sight in the court of Shivba. Everyone had realized Abaji Sondev's blunder and the code of ethics and conduct that he had violated. Shivba saw the young lady and immediately ordered her release with respect and honour. Mulla Ahmed's daughter-in-law was sent to her home with the escorts to ensure her safety and well-being. Abaji Sondev was repentful and apologized for his conduct.

Shivba reprimanded his Sardars and issued a stern warning that in future, during raids or war with the enemy, no woman shall be made to suffer or treated as booty.

Belvadi Mallamma

Mallamma was the daughter of King Madhulinga Nayaka Sodhe Kingdom. She had married Ishaprabhu Desai, Prince of Belvadi and came to be known as Belvadi Mallamma.

During Shivba's Dakshin Digvijay or the conquest or expansion in South India in 1678, Ishaprabhu challenged the mighty Shivba by committing plunders of the transport bullocks of the Maratha army. Shivba had already concluded his Southern campaign with his massive force of thirty thousand cavalry (soldiers on horses), twenty thousand infantry (soldiers on foot) and had no plans of invading Belavadi for any reason. Ishaprabhu was defeated in a battle caused by him and died but his brave wife Mallamma unbelievably fought against the powerful Maratha army for twenty-seven days in defense.

Belavadi Mallamma was however defeated and captured and brought before Shivba. Mallamma asked for a truce which Shivba agreed to. Shivba treated the brave warrior like Belavadi Mallamma with great respect even though she had been defeated. Shivba set her free, patronized her territory and gave back her kingdom as a mark of respect for a woman like Mallamma. Shivba's humility, respect and appreciation had a tremendous influence on Mallamma. Shivba's high calibre and conduct towards women and his people had deeply impressed Belavadi Mallamma.

Mallamma told Shivba that one of his commanders Sakhuji Gaikwar had misbehaved with her after her capture. Shivba ordered to bring the Sakhuji before him and on proving of his guilt, punished Sakhuji where both his eyes were gouged out.

Mallamma had a four-month son at the time of her capture and subsequent release. She had such a high regard for Shivba that she ordered a stone sculpture to be made at Yadvad, about ten kilometers north of Dharwad in Karnataka to commemorate Shivba's chivalry. The finely carved sculpture of Shivba is on a black granite slab divided in two parts. The upper half shows Shivba riding a horse in his royal attire holding a sword in his right hand and a shield in the left, and a dog next to the horse. On the lower panel, Shivba is seen holding a bowl in his hands and feeding milk to Mallamma's infant baby whom Mallamma has placed in Shivba's lap as a token of his assurance of safety to her. Mallamma is also seen standing nearby, holding bow and arrow. Such was the high regard for Shivba shown even by the captured queen for the profound respect he had for women, which he learnt from his mother Jijabai.

Rai Bagan

Savitribai Deshmukh, also known by her title Rai Bagan or Rai Baghin ('Royal Tigress'), was a female Mughal general under Aurangzeb. She was the widow of the Mughal sardar Raje Udaram Deshmukh of Mahur jagir in Deccan. In Battle of Samugarh, she helped Aurangzeb in the battle against his elder brother Dara Shikhoh, which paved his way to become the emperor. Aurangzeb was impressed and conferred upon her the royal title of Rai Bagan.

Rai Bagan also aided Aurangzeb's uncle Shaista Khan in the Mughal campaign against Swarajya. Shahista Khan had appointed Kartalab Khan and Raibagan to attack Konkan, which was under Swarajya, with the force of twenty thousand soldiers. Kartalab Khan and Rai Bagan chose the path of Kurvanda Ghat where Shivba and his army were waiting for them in the forest near Umberkhind (Umber Gorge) which was approximately 9 miles long. In the Battle of Umberkhind, as Mughals entered the Umberkhind and came ahead, they heard the blowing horns and were stunned by sudden attack of arrows of around three-four hundred Maratha archers and swordsmen led by Shivba himself. Shivba was sitting on a horse with his bow slung on the right shoulder.

Kartalab Khan, Rai Bagan along with other Mughal soldiers tried to retreat in emergency but the forest was thick and the Marathas were prepared. Mughals couldn't even see their enemy and were killed with arrows and swords. Rai Bagan had the presence of mind so she advised Kartalab Khan to surrender to Shivba and ask for mercy. Maratha army of around thousand men defeated the Mughals with twenty thousand soldiers. As soon as truce was called, Shivba showed mercy. Rai Bagan was let off with respect even though she was a Mughal general. Rai Bagan saw Shivba's bravery and his conduct towards women so praised Shivba in the court of Shahista Khan.

In January 1664, Rai Bagan again confronted Shivba during the Battle of Surat. Rai Bagan again lost the battle and was captured. But Shivba showed courtesy and great hospitality towards her. Rai Bagan was honoured and sent back to her jagir.

Shaista Khan

Shivba had an impeccable reputation about his moral conduct towards women even among his fiercest enemies like Mughals and other Sultanates. They knew that well that Shivba would not disrespect or cause any harm to women, saints, religion and religious texts. Many revered Shivba to be the protector of good people and cows. And such a reputation was not earned by any King or ruler of that time. Shivba's enemies, no doubt, were against him and even disliked him but none of the historical records show that he was ever said to be deviated from his good and moral conduct towards women.

Shaista Khan came to Pune and camped for almost three years with strength of around fifty thousand soldiers, camels, horses and elephants. Shaista Khan had his family along with him as he made Lal Mahal, Shivba's house in Pune his base.

On 5th April 1665, Shivba and his men raided Lal Mahal to attack Shaista Khan who was ruining Pune and harassing the people. The women in Shaista Khan's family extinguished the oil lamps so invaders could not find Shaista Khan. As soon as Shaista Khan came to know that Marathas were there to kill him, he took refuge behind women to make them a shield as he knew Shivba would not attack a woman. Shivba however managed to drive Shaista Khan out of his hiding but Shaista Khan ran towards the window in darkness. Shivba swung his sword to slice Shaista Khan but a very fortunate Shaista Khan just lost his three fingers and came out alive of this attack by jumping out of window. Shivba and his men escaped safely.

As the chaos settled, Mughal women claimed that a daughter from the family was missing. Shaista Khan calmed the women by saying that he was confident that no woman would be taken away by Shivba. It was indeed true, as the missing girl hid herself in a huge pot when the bloody raid ensued and came out safe to her family. Shaista Khan, who camped in Pune for three years, hastily left Pune in three days.

Khafi Khan, the bitter and hostile critic of Shivba, had his father in service of Aurangzeb. He described the treatment of women prisoners by Shivba as,

"If a Hindu or Muslim woman fell into the hands of his men no one had the courage to look at her with an evil eye and Shivaji strove to protect her till her heirs came and rescued her by paying a ransom according to their means."

(Khafi Khan in Mutakhab-ul Lubab, translated).

Shivba called every woman as his sister or mother and there was no such ruler or king who kept the moral code of conduct as high as he did. There is no such precedent of having a King who was as brave, powerful and as morally enriched as Shivba. This attribute of Shivba alone won him hearts and respect from all sections of caste, creed, class, religion, and geographical regions of Bharatvarsh.

9. SHIVBA AND SAHYADRI

Shivba spent his childhood in Sahyadri. The love for the motherland, sense of freedom, and desire for well-being of people ran in the veins of Shivba. Sahyadri was like a second mother for Shivba who protected its child under any circumstances that he faced in his entire life. He was born in Sahyadri and lived in its lap till he was alive. Sahyadri was in the very being of Shivba no matter what he did. He was a son of a commander and while he became a pious king and saviour of people, obedient son and a great ruler, he always had Sahyadri by his side.

Sahyadri, or the Western Ghats, is a mountain range that covers a stretch of 1,600 kms (990 miles) and runs parallel to the western coast of the Indian peninsula, starting near the south of the Tapti or also known as Tapi river in Gujarat.

Sahyadri crosses across through the States of Gujarat, Maharashtra, Goa, Karnataka, Kerala and

Tamil Nadu ending at Marunthuvazh Malai in Kanyakumari District, near the southern tip of India. It is sometimes called the Great Escarpment of India. Sahyadri is older than the Himalayas and has rich natural resources in its vast spread. Sahyadri receives a very heavy rainfall and is home to a large number of species of animals.

Sahyadri, with the average elevation of around 1,200 m (3,900 ft) is not for the faint-hearted. It is extremely perilous and difficult to scale but also has serene beauty which attracts people and animals to inhabit in it. Sahyadri is ancient name for the mountain range considered to be the one of the seven sacred mountain ranges of the ancient Indian. The word Sahyadri is derived from two words, Sahya (tolerant) and Adri (mountain). Shiva Purana mentions Sahyadri as one of the places where Rudraksha is grown. Sahyadri Khanda a part of the great Skanda purana describes the rivers, terrain, and the mountains of Sahyadri in detail along with other important stories. Sahyadri ranges are older than the Himalayas.

Sahyadri passes through a major part of Maharashtra from the highest peak of Kalsubai near Nashik in the north which is the highest point in Maharashtra at elevation of 1,646 meters (5,400 ft), to Amboli Ghat in the south of Maharashtra. Sahyadri is inhabited in Maharashtra by the people on the western part of the State. Sahyadri largely influence the Indian monsoon weather patterns by intercepting the monsoon winds that flow in from the south-west during late summers. Sahyadri ranges runs from North along the western edge of the Deccan Plateau to the South. Sahyadri sets apart the plateau from a narrow coastal plain called the Western Coastal Plains along the Arabian Sea. The Western Coastal Plains is 50 kilometers (31 mi) in width strip of coastal plain between the west coast of India and the Western Ghats hills. The plains are located between the Western Ghats and the Arabian Sea starting from Gujarat in the north and end at Kanyakumari in Tamil Nadu covering the States of Gujarat, Maharashtra, Goa, Karnataka, Kerala and a small part of Tamil Nadu.

The Western plains consists of three sections, namely, the northern part of the coast called the Konkan (Mumbai to Goa), the central stretch is called the Kanara or the Karavali, while the southern stretch is referred to as the Malabar Coast. The state of Maharashtra can be categorized into five basic geographical regions - *Konkan, Desh, Khandesh, Marathwada* and *Vidarbha.* Desh or Maharashtra Desh is a historical region of the west-central Deccan Plateau which can be easily identified as Division of Pune.

In the sixteenth and seventeenth century, the population of Maharashtra was very less and most of the parts of the land were covered with dense forests.

The edge on the western side of the Deccan plateau received a low rainfall which was more or less uncertain. The peasants only could assure themselves of a good return on the narrow margins of along the few rivers. The land under the scarce rainfall remained untilled and unwatered which made cultivation a bare source of subsistence. The rice cultivation was impossible in such conditions. Peasants could bet for a very small quantity of wheat and barley which could be rewarding if more quantities of them could be cultivated. Only the millets like Jawari, Bajra, Ragi, Maize could grow as they tough and could sustain in dry conditions and less water. They were called as hardy millets. But sometimes even millets would get scorched by sun and scanty rainfall resulting in famine which would perish people and cattles in large numbers.

The abundant forest in Maharashtra naturally made the sections in the region which separated people and thus made them self-reliant. There was no kingdom or the big trade markets thriving before Shivba. The people found a safe haven from the Northern invasions due to the inhospitable geography that this region possessed. The westwards expansion of invaders broke at the foothills. Some invasions were so unprofitable that making an endurance to percolate their armies deep within was not attempted after a while. There were only some trades and pilgrims which took place from this region.

Sahyadri is in the minds and overall being of people inhabiting here. It has engraved a sense of high self-esteem and pride which can never be eroded. It is tough to survive surroundings that have shaped men in the region to be self-sufficient. The tendency of surviving in this terrain has depleted the fear of being subjugated. Terrains of Sahyadri have moulded its people into the toughest race to ever survive and form their own kingdom and later rule almost the whole Indian subcontinent. Sahyadri is the mother to all the women who gave birth to the men of greatest valour. Women also gave birth to the spirit of dignity in the child to live with honour even in the face of adversity. She defined how men lived and died defending their motherland from the invasions.

This may not have always been about the fight against the invaders before they came to Bharat. The people in Sahyadri thrived as the rich natural resources they were bestowed upon never seemed to fade away. Marathas were hardened by the strenuous conditions which built strong muscles, resilient souls and stout hearts which found great opportunities in the then warring kingdoms. They were granted high pays, noble ranks and good reputation owing to their capabilities in the military combats. The Sultanates were always at the lookout of these stalwarts who were loyal, trustworthy and immensely dedicated to their duties. Although, not all Maratha commanders were not handsomely paid but the powerful ones like Shahaji Raje commanded great respect and were able to maintain their own troops, horses and big estates.

Marathas were the proud farmers or peasants who after the sowing in the farms melted their ploughs to make the swords after the festival of Dussera and leave for military campaigns till the harvesting season arrived. This way they yielded what they could as farmers and made more than what they needed for their subsistence through military campaigns. Although, these campaigns did not make them a big fortune but it ensured that they had enough to maintain themselves and their servants.

Military undertakings came naturally to Marathas due to their physical strength and mental tenacity but they had no commonality when it came to political aspirations. There was no kingdom or the ruler to whom they could mutually owe their allegiance so they had a split in their loyalties towards different Courts where they flourished effortlessly. The valour and military efficiency were put to good use by the Sultanates for their own interests but there was no welfare of the state ever intended by these rulers. Maratha officers knew this and also knew how their people are exploited but all they could do was wish that they had a cause to lay their lives for. This cause, worthy to strive and perish for, was to be served by Shivba in the near future.

Maratha people's inborn dedication and love for their independence was protected by the terrains of Sahyadri. The mighty Sahyadri provided hills with steep edges and smooth rock walls surrounding the top of the hill making them insurmountable. The high peaks were shielded portions, upright and rigid, which formed natural fortresses. The summit to these hills gave the access to natural strongholds which could enable strategic control on the region. The springs of water and the water collected during the rains in tanks or reservoirs of water made it possible to live on the forts throughout the year.

Maratha people in ancient Maharashtra were extremely simple and worked hard with their hands. They were humble and down to earth and did not believe in accumulating wealth in gold and silver. The richness was often displayed in heaps of grains and people hired for labour and such richness was usually with traders or *Saavkars* ('money lenders'). There was no filthy display of wealth and means of pleasure like the over-polished decadents of Mughals and other Sultanates. Marathas valued people and the simplicity of life while he kept their heads high with pride and glory of their dignified independence. The Chinese traveller Yuan Chwang also known as Hiuen Tsang or Xuanzang had visited India during 629-645 AD and went to various parts of India. Yuan Chwang also visited the Maratha country and wrote about the people as under:

> *"The manners of the Marathas are simple and honest. They are proud and reserved. If any one is kind to them he may be sure of their gratitude, but if any one injures them, they will take their revenge and risk their life to wipe out dishonour. If any one in distress appeals to them, they will leave aside all thoughts of self in their anxiety to help. Even if they have an insult to avenge, they never fail to warn their enemy. In battle if they pursue the fugitives, they always spare all who surrender. These men love study and there are many heretics among them."*

- Yuan Chwang, 7th century AD.

Shivba found a great asset of Sahyadri to his side as he was establishing Swarajya and got into a fierce conflict against the Sultanates and other European powers which were rising strong. Sahyadri was instrumental in building a kingdom around the steady and arduous forts which even brought the mighty armies to their knees. There were taller mountains, higher peaks and bigger topographies in India but none were as challenging as the laps of Sahyadri.

Shivba, a born leader, knew his men well that they were self-reliant, courageous, perseverant, and were straightforward but intensely dedicated to the noble cause of Swarajya. Mavala(s), a name for the brave men of the hilly region to the west of present-day Pune in Maharashtra, were a perfect combination of courage, smartness and power of endurance, in their military tactics and combative skills. Their strength was the mastery to plan and execute surprises and night attacks on the enemies and making tactical changes in a whisk and adapting smoothly to the surroundings made them suitable for the battle against the large armies of Sultanates. The formidable hills-forts served as a quick refuge against the attack from the enemies. The Mavalas would flee when there would be a massive attack to these forts and return with a tough resistance which would cause wreck on the enemy fronts and scatter their troops.

The terrains of Sahyadri were unlike the Gangetic plains where the entire region could be captured by heavy cavalry attack by campaigning for a long time when needed. Sahyadri was not friendly to the outsiders even in large numbers who would wear out easily. While the natives were able to battle with a small number of men and keep recovering and hold their position.

The geographical factors have historically changed the fortunes in war and battles and no able general would turn his blind eye towards it, no matter how large his army was and how big treasure was he able to carry. As latest as in 1812, the French emperor and military commander Napoleon Bonaparte crossed Neman River and invaded Russia with a Grande army of more than five hundred thousand. Russians just retreated to the interiors causing a long march and lack of supplies and distribution networks. Grande army encountered the harsh winters of Russia for which they were not prepared and lost three hundred thousand soldiers and later retreated to France in despair and severely weakened. It was later said that the Grande army of Napoleon was defeated not by Russian Generals but by 'Le général hiver' or 'General Winter', the harsh winter of Russia. Napoleon failed to assess the terrain of Russia and faced the biggest defeat of all time.

Similarly, Aurangzeb and his huge army marched upon Deccan to conquer Swarajya without properly assessing the terrain and the peril involved in doing so. Aurangzeb's commanders would boast that they would conquer Shivba's territories. Shivba wrote a letter to the army officers of Aurangzeb slamming them for their tall claims. Shivba wrote Persian or Farsi words, *'Samande Talaash, Beqayaas'* meaning in the context that they can't even think of running 'an imaginary horse' in his territory and still they claimed to conquer it. It was no wonder that the Mughals always challenged Shivba to come in open field for a battle but in vain.

The powerful Adilshahi General Afzal Khan took the challenge upon himself in the Court of Adilshah

Sultanate to capture Shivba, dead or alive, as according to them he had menaced the territory of Adilshah. Afzal Khan came to Wai at the foothills of Mahabaleshwar. Shivba with his wit and tactics brought Afzal Khan to meet him in person leaving behind his army and accompanied only with ten bodyguards from both the sides and killed him in a hand-to-hand combat. Afzal Khan was overconfident and did not understand Sahyadri as deeply as Shivba did. As soon as Afzal Khan climbed down the Ghat of *Radtondi* (which literally means Cry face owing to its difficulty) above the area of Javali, his death was certain. Afzal Khan had to eliminate elephants and canons from carrying it down to Javali and then Pratapgad as it was a perilous terrain. By the time, Afzal Khan reached Javali to reach Pratapgad, he was already trapped in inescapable range of mighty Sahyadri. The battle of Pratapgad is a classic example of tactful victory over the foe by his sole placement in hostile terrain.

Shivba developed *Ganimi Kaava* or Guerrilla Warfare, which is an unconventional tactical warfare where a small number of soldiers use ambush, sabotage, raid and other tactics to fight with a large and more equipped army. Ganimi Kaava was the major strength of Marathas to vanquish the enemies with very little or no loss of men and horses and significant gain of war booty. Mughals lost their treasure, horses, military equipment and even their military costumes in the sudden attacks of Marathas. The military costumes played a remarkable role for Maratha spies and soldiers in disguising as Mughal officers and entering their camps unnoticed to collect information and sometimes to cause ruckus and unrest among Mughals.

Although, Marathas were gruesome in open field battles and Shivba has led some of them himself being on the battlefield. Shivba fought his first battle near Purandar at an age of fifteen years. After killing Afzal Khan at Pratapgad, Shivba led his army and conquered territory till Panhala Fort near present day Kolhapur. Maratha armies faced the Bijapur army under the commander Rustam-e-Zaman in the battle of Kolhapur in the aftermath of battle of Pratapgad where Afzal Khan was killed. Shivba himself led the charge of the battle from the center. The baffled Bijapur army was on the verge of retreat but before anyone else their commander Rustam-e-Zaman himself fled the battlefield. Similarly, the Marathas fought valiantly in open field battles at Battle of Salher, Battle of Vani-Dindori where Shivba himself led his army wearing Baghtar (body armour) and Ghugi (head armour) and defeated the Mughal army led by Daud Khan, Ikhilas Khan and Sangram Khan on his way after sacking Surat and capturing a huge treasure.

Even during the reign of Sambhaji Maharaj, the exemplary warrior, second Chhatrapati of Swarajya and the elder son of Shivba, the Aurangzeb was presumptuous that he will conquer the territory of Swarajya without a hitch and started the campaign by the storm. Aurangzeb chose the so-called easiest to capture fort called Ramshej near Nashik to boost the morale of his men. He appointed commander Shahbuddin Khan and provided him forty thousand soldiers and strong artillery for the onslaught on Ramshej fort. Shahbuddin Khan claimed to capture the fort within a few hours. The handful of six hundred Marathas fiercely resisted the attack and defended the fort against the heavy attack of the Mughals. The fort did not have cannons but Marathas made cannons with animal skin and wood. Aurangzeb changed commanders in his bid to capture the 'easiest' fort. The commanders tried bizarre means like building a high wooden platform, calling black magician to get rid of ghosts, none of which ever worked. The fort resisted the siege for seven long years after which it was given away by Marathas as they found no reason to hold on any longer. Sahyadri bestowed advantage to its natives who were able to put up a fight where they would otherwise perish.

Mughals suffered miserably as they never got the gist of how Sahyadri, the mighty single nature force, stood in their way of conquer. They never got past this force which enabled natives to lead respectful lives without being enslaved ever. Aurangzeb, the most powerful Mughal emperor, had defeated all other Sultanates in a matter of a few years. He aspired to bring territory from Kandahar to Tanjavur under the Mughal Sultanate but Sahyadri and its son Shivba ruined his shrewd expansion plans. Aurangzeb's mindset is clear from the fact that he left his capital Agra carrying his treasure, *Janankhana* (consorts and other women), precious belongings, artworks, army, cavalry, artillery, camels and personal belongings along to Deccan. Aurangzeb was aware that it was 'long-drawn battle' to go the Maratha country to conquer it. In 1707, Aurangzeb, died miserably defeated by Marathas, at Bhingar near Ahmednagar, Maharashtra after the long twenty-seven years battle with Marathas. He could not conquer Sahyadri and he could not subdue the free-spirited Marathas.

Shivba knew that on day Aurangzeb would invade Deccan and try to defeat and vanquish Swarajya. In order to avert the complete conquer, Shivba had a strategic vision that he had built three hundred and fifty forts in Maharashtra and even if his one fort fought for a period of one year against the Mughals, Aurangzeb would require a life of three hundred and fifty years to conquer his kingdom.

Shivba wandered day and night in the Sahyadri as a child as he played with his peers. He studied the terrain like it was a book. He got aware of the routes in Sahyadri like he knew he would blaze through someday on his mighty horse. Shivba sub-consciously feel under his tiny feet, the hard basalt rocks and could hear the heartbeat of this land. Everything that he became, he became one with the enormous Sahyadri.

Shivba did not remain far away from Sahyadri for a long time. He went to Agra for a visit to Aurangzeb under the treaty of Purandar and for his conquest of Dakshin Digvijay but returned to Deccan soon after. Shivba stayed near Sahyadri as a calf would always be around the cow. Sahyadri had enchanted a mantra of independence and dignity in the ears of its children. Sahyadri is the phenomenon of bravery and resilience, which stayed in the souls of its people till their last breath. Sahyadri is not only a geographical aspect of this great country but indeed a jewel in its crown.

10. SHIVBA'S OATH OF SWARAJYA

Shivba was growing up around his mother and his friends in Sahyadri. The hostile situation around Jijabai and Shivba had relatively calmed down as Shahaji Raje had politically stabilized under Adil Shah. Shahaji Raje was sent as a deputy of Randulla Khan to subjugate Raya Rayal who was posing threats to Adil Shah. Shahaji Raje was handed over the jagirs of the provinces which were won over by him in this campaign which lasted for two or three years. The jagirs of Akalkote, Bagalkote, Bengaluru, Vaskote, Balapore and Shirta were conquered by Shahaji Raje. Shahaji earned the high favour of Randulla Khan by his dedication to the conquests.

The Sultan was pleased with Shahaji's valour and gave him the conquered provinces of Akalkote, Bagalkote, Bengaluru, Vaskote, Balapore and Shirta in jagir. Soon after, the districts of Ratanpore, Deogad, Kanakgiri, and Rajdurg were added to his jagir, and his

Maharashtra jagir got the addition of Indapar, Baramati, and Maval. Shahaji Raje was also conferred the Deshmukhi of twenty-two villages in the Karhad district.

Shahaji Raje had found a position in the Court where his skills were valued. Bijapur Court believed that Shahaji Raje was a competent and a loyal commander. There was no other person who would administer the newly acquired territories for Adil Shah so he was conferred with the high post where he was in control of the provinces given to him as jagirs. The new territories were in disorder and under misrule which only Shahaji Raje could bring in order. Shahaji Raje being a fine statesman was able to bring about the administration that Bijapur needed in the acquired provinces. He, however, did not harass the natives of Karnataka and instead developed a friendly bond with them and took a great care of the people. He was meticulous in sending the revenue quota to the Sultan and earned a good surplus to himself.

Shahaji Raje was very well-versed with finances and brought the finance clerks or *karkuns* from Maharashtra and developed a revenue system which helped the people and also brought impressive revenue stream to the provinces. Shahaji Raje later captured Thanjavur and Tiruchirappalli and annexed it to his jagirs under the conformity with Bijapur. Shahaji Raje had eventually earned such popularity and the grateful affection of his people that in the event of collision with Bijapur Sultan, he would be easily able to achieve support from the natives. The people of Karanataka even at present have deeds of grants and other *Sanads* to his subjects which came directly from the 'durbar of Raja Shahaji Bhonsale' and not from Sultan.

When he turned eleven years old, Shahaji Raje summoned Jijabai and Shivba to Bengaluru to stay with him at his royal residence. Shivba saw that the city of Bengaluru had a very strong fortification. The palaces were tall and high and were white lime washed. There were artistic sculptors on the palaces which suited well. He could see the parva birds (red-breasted flycatcher) all around and also hear peacocks screams in the city.

There were hawkers in the streets for selling sorts of things to people. The city had a large number of wells. There were crossroads where water fountains were installed. The huge trees in the parks gave ample shade on the ground. The houses had large paintings on its walls which was captivating for the eyes. The horse stables were built using stones which were painted in different colours making them look fascinating.

Shivba saw that the canons were installed atop the bastions in parts of the city which were well-guarded by the soldiers under the command of Shahaji Raje. There was a ditch or trench which was filled with water so it looked very entrancing. There were beautiful flower gardens at many corners and the city had magnificent temples within. Shahaji Raje was ruling the city like a king for whom the people had very high regards. Shivba's elder brother Sambhaji, seven years elder to Shivba, was also there at Bengaluru residing with his father. Jijabai was elated to meet her elder son who had been away from her for a period of more than eleven or twelve years.

Sambhaji, remarkably, was the name of Shivba's uncle viz. Shahaji Raje's cousin. Shahaji Raje named his son as Sambhaji who was killed at the age of thirty-two in the battle of Kanakgiri due to the treachery of Afzal Khan. Shivba named his elder son as Sambhaji, who became the second Chhatrapati of Swarajya. Sambhaji name was closely attached to Shivba's family and re-kindled the sentiments as they named a son after the one in the previous generation.

In Bengaluru royal residence of Shahaji Raje, there was an elephant at the doorstep which amused Shivba. There were thousands of majestic horses in the royal stable. Shahaji Raje's influence was growing by leaps and bounds and as he prospered day by day, his power grew in parallel.

Shivba was very keen and observant and was fond of examining the qualities of horses and elephants while visiting military depots and magazines. Shivba behaved with remarkable etiquettes and courtesy towards eminent persons and he also endeavored to acquire knowledge by the tactful method in which he inquired into the various subjects. Shivba all his life hated vice and luxury. His qualities soon won him the high regard of the nobles.

The nobles were so impressed by the young Shivba's manners that on one occasion they spoke of him with great regard to the Sultan. Sultan expressed a desire to see Shivba, the promising son of his noted General. Shahaji Raje was obliged to introduce Shivba to the Adil Shah's court. Shivba was not pleased with the prospect of a meeting the Sultan and pleaded to his father with great modesty and submission to excuse him from the ordeal. Shivba was not inclined to flatter the Sultan and his men who were so mean and brazen in their ways against the Hindus. Shivba was sure that he could not tolerate the disdain they had for his religion.

Shivba was stubborn and was not willing to submit before the cruel Mohammedans who ruined the life of his people and had covered their hands with sins. He was not able to reconcile with the fact that he would prostrate himself before the Sultan whom he considered was one of the Mohammedans who desecrated Hindu shrines and burned their holy scriptures. It was not an easy task for Shahaji Raje to persuade the young Shivba that since they serve the Islamic rulers, they have to conduct themselves within a certain degree of compliance to look after their interest and prevention of conflict. Shivba was not ready to abide by before the Islamic kings who invaded our lands and violated our women for the sheer greed of power and pleasure. It was only when Jijabai herself intervened and explained to Shivba that it was not only the inappropriate timing but also the method in which a resistance could be made against the Sultanates. Jijabai was the one who instilled the passion of independence in the young Shivba so her intervention was bound to persuade Shivba to flow the trail which his father has indicated till the time he carves his own path. Shivba was aware that self-rule or Swarajya was deeply aspired project of his father so if he had stipulated the course, he might as well subscribe to it for a time being. Shivba had no other choice as well given his parents had persuaded him so he reluctantly agreed to accompany his father to the durbar.

Shivba would often see the sights of cow-slaughter, as he passed the streets which infuriated him and made his blood boil but he resisted the strong urge to thrash the slayer of cows.

Shahaji Raje had instructed Shivba about the court etiquette of saluting the Sultan by bowing down to the ground at the presence of Sultan. But rebellious Shivba only made a slight Salaam (salutation) and seated himself by his father. The Sultan observed the boy accompanied by Shahaji Raje so he enquired about him. Sultan was told by Shahaji Raje that it was his son's first visit to the durbar. The Sultan presented jewels and robes of honour to the young Shivba as a mark of his acknowledgment. Shivba as soon as he returned home, discarded the robe and had a bath.

Shivba accompanied his father to the durbar several times, but every time, he made only a slight Salaam and took his seat by his father. This was noticed by the Sultan so he questioned Shivba upfront about it. Shivba, who had a great presence of mind, told the Sultan that he was repeatedly reminded to make his salute according to the etiquette of prostration but at the last moment he forgot it and made the salaam as usual. The Sultan burst into a feat laughter listening to Shivba's witty reply.

Shivba could no longer bear the sight of cow-slaughter on his way to the palace so he told his father that he will no longer attend the durbar. The butchers had the beef and head of cattles hanging on the slaughter houses in full display, even by hawkers at booths opposite the palace gates. Shivba was offended by this abhorrent spectacle but suppressed his urge to act against it. He openly protested about this to his father. Once it happened that a butcher was about to slaughter a cow at the very moment when Shivba was passing by on his way to the palace. Shivba caught hold of the butcher and delivered blows to him to rescue the cow. This news spread in the market and even reached the

Sultan's ears. Shahaji Raje was perplexed by this. So, he approached his friend, Mir Jumla, an old friend at the court who took this up with the Sultan. The Sultan was told that his Hindu subjects were offended by the open cow-slaughter in front of the palace gates and it was only Sultan who could rectify this. Sultan, after a careful hearing, ordered the butchers not to carry out slaughter in the vicinity of the palace and migrate out of the city in an isolated place in the South.

Shivba began to attend the durbar again with his father. One day a butcher came with the basket full of cow flesh to sell near the palace and just then Shivba and some of his friends came on their horses. As soon as Shivba saw the butcher, he drew his sword and cut down the butcher. There was a complaint by the butcher's wife but the Sultan defended the act as it was the breach his own edict on this issue. Even then, there was a discontent with the locals that Sultan sided against the honest Mohammedans. Shahaji Raje tried to reason with Shivba and sought Jijabai for her opinion. They inferred that they cannot change the nature of their boy and maybe his defiance is the indication of his suitability to bid for the rise of a new self-ruled kingdom of Hindus.

Shahaji Raje realized this was his opportunity that his scion was aptly equipped for the outset of his dream of achieving principality which he had attempted so far. Shahaji Raje had appointed one Dadoji Konddev, a

Brahmin loyal and capable minister to administer the jagirs at Pune and Supa. Shahaji and Jijabai thought it was most appropriate to send Shivba to rule over the jagirs and learn the administration and know his subjects. Shivba was given two thousand *hons*, a thousand cavalry, *astha-pradhan* mandal (ministers) and other necessities for the outset of his ambitious enterprise.

Shivba wandered the twelve Mavalas or the sunset land and surveyed its every nook and corner in order to assess his territory. He endlessly met people, understood their lifestyle, their difficulties and their primary expectations from the administrators. The Pune district that Dadaji took over was in unfortunately ruined condition. The six years of warfare had nearly destroyed the land. The invading armies left the ruins to be further exploited more by the robber chiefs. As the province was passed on from Nizamshah to Bijapur, there was no rule that had been established by then.

Shivba had realized the mammoth effort of human spirit that will be required to accomplish the noble task of establishing Swarajya. Shivba had said

हे हिंदवी स्वराज्य व्हावे ही श्रींची इच्छा

('It is Almight's wish that this may be a Hindu kingdom)

Shivba and his companions, who he had found in Maval, had resolved to build a kingdom for justice, independence and protection of their motherland. They already called it Swarajya. One fine day of 27th April 1645, Shivba and his companions went to Raireshwar, located in Bhor Taluka near Pune. The place was not very accessible and safe for the rebellious meeting. The young boys went to the mystical temple of Shivba for taking the oath of Swarajya.

Shivba took his sword and gave a cut to his little finger for the Arghya or libation by his blood over the Shivalinga ('symbol of Shiva') and took the oath of establishing Swarajya. This was the historic moment in the entire history of civilization of people on Deccan Plateau.

Shivba was indeed blessed by the Almighty. All that he manifested for the people to save them from clutches of slavery and subjugation came true and a pious kingdom Swarajya saw the light of the day, under the auspices of Goddess Bhavani, Goddess Shivai, mother Jijabai and his exceptional General-father, Shahaji Raje. The oath before the Shiva came true and then followed a series of heroics of Shivba which history witnessed with all the pride and glory.

ABOUT THE AUTHOR

Vikrant Shinde is an Advocate-on-record of Supreme Court of India, practicing also at Bombay High Court and Courts in Pune. He has a law practice of more than sixteen years. He did his Bachelor's in Law degree from Yashwantrao Chavan Law College, Pune (University of Pune) and has a Master degree in Business Laws from National Law School of India University, Bengaluru. He heads a law firm named Virtue Resolute, based in Pune. He frequently delivers talks on Legal Awareness and general issues at various organizations.

Vikrant has had a keen interest in history since the time when he was in primary school. He is an enthusiast particularly of Maratha history, Indian Culture and nuances of Hinduism. His learnings come from the fact that he grew up near Sahyadri ranges and like any other child, heard the stories of Chhatrapati Shivaji Maharaj & Chhatrapati Sambhaji Maharaj. Forts of Maharashtra and other States have always fascinated him and encouraged him to find more about the hidden treasures of history. Vikrant can be reached via email for any communication for official purposes of this book at ivikrantshinde@gmail.com.

www.ingramcontent.com/pod-product-compliance
Lightning Source LLC
Chambersburg PA
CBHW050017170726
48282CB00025B/441
9789360398774